TEMPLE OF DESTINY

FAITH IN ONESELF

IS GREATER THAN ANY FAITH ON EARTH

NEERAJ SINGHVI

First Published 2009
Second Edition 2021

ISBN 978-16-7898-557-8

Dedicated to my family who has been a great support to me during this Endeavour.

I also owe it to the fishes.

Index:

Preface

I have been extremely fortunate in being able to write this book. This book helps one understand the reasons behind the various forms of life, the birth and death of every living creature on this planet and the life support systems that have been created by the almighty for making life possible on this planet-Earth. This is also the focus of this book.

At a time, when I was trying to set up my business, I used to watch a fishbowl with a few fishes, in my house. One day while watching it closely, thoughts started percolating inside me about the integration of the mind, body and soul and its inter-connection with the planets and universe. Somewhere, I was being told that the fishes were trying to teach me things which no one else could and thus started my journey of writing this book so I could bring it in front of millions of people who I think, would also like to know about it.

This book is a story that starts in the United States of America and swiftly changes to the Indian sub-continent. Harrod and Guruji are the two principal characters who play the central role in the entire story, and it revolves around the journey which only the fishes can teach. **The story portrays 4 important connections or cycles in the life of a man.**

The story revolves around the thought that the entire world is inter-linked wirelessly and more so by the sixth sense, i.e., the power to communicate with each other without speaking, watching or hearing. It shows the fantastic bondage of one person with the other which is so exhilarating. Sometimes it is the non-binding factors between two persons or two regions or two living and non-living systems that provide an inexplicable intrigue. It also shows the pen-ultimate bonding between the male and female varieties of every living species which transforms the planet every day, the fusion which is providing the life-making mechanisms that are preparing the world to move ahead daily. It is so meticulously carved with so much refinery and precision, that it is almost impossible to fathom the magic that works here.

Not that humankind cannot understand and recreate this inner-self, but it is the inexplicable built-in systems entwined in the entire world that make it so impossible for humankind to perceive. I believe we have provided humankind with all the means and capabilities to interact, interview and inter-twine the complete mystery. Of course, I also believe that humans will never appreciate the whole mastermind behind this, even when they get to know about the revelation.

This book is about taking action, a thrilling experience in the world of thoughts, a simplistic adventure and an approach to one's own life. It is on a creation beyond self. This book tries to deliver the significance of our lives and their co-existence with nature.

While writing the book, everything that is a problem in the world has just passed through my mind. Although the book does not directly refer to these points, I have found that natural factors are a big cause of the destruction of the earth and a lot of it directly results from the plans that man has made for himself. We find natural disasters such as cyclones hitting countries, whales being hunted, cities getting flooded, earthquakes destroying properties and life, industrial gases polluting the atmosphere, plastics being thrown away indiscriminately, fire ravaging forests and towns, oil getting scarcer, tropical storms hitting coastlines, heavy morning fogs, floods and cyclones destroying villages and crops, glaciers around the world melting, people marching against climate change, ozone layers depleting, energy-guzzling firms, unprecedented carbon emissions, animals being hunted, aquatic life being threatened, drugs being grown and traded, various kinds of deadly flu and virus coming into existence, wars taking place between countries and between people, are few of the only things in the headlines of various daily newspapers and news channels worldwide. Therefore, I found it imperative to showcase the direct connection of man with nature and beyond so that we understand and rectify our ways of working to suit nature.

While we look at these, we also find efforts being made by various communities and governments around the world to wriggle out of all the problems that the world is facing. Solutions are being worked out as bio-degradable products which can free the earth of plastics; bio-fuels being extracted from plants to remove our over-dependence on natural oil; wind and solar power being exploited to remove air pollution; efforts to contain carbon emissions through carbon credits being explored; generation of electricity from sources other than coal and various other measures being taken to counter the adverse effects of the wrongdoings of humans on this planet so that future generations can still enjoy living on Earth.

The need of the hour is to address these issues on a war footing, and this book through its story, explains the process to rectify our system at its roots. What I have mentioned above comes from the roots of our very own value systems? If we can rectify these, then we can save the earth from the miseries to which it is being subjected.

In the entire story, there are a few poems that will also help explain the mysteries of life. Every poem is self-explanatory, but to provide its true value, I have juxtaposed them with the relevant topics. **This book has no connection with any religion and is a story that helps explain in simple terms our purpose of coming into this world.**

I would like to sum up the book asunder.

It is the Way

The History of nature

Sheds down,

As winter sets in.

What seems to blossom every day,

Blows off,

To un-distinguished places.

But! not for long,

As Spring sets in

Bringing with it

The most joyful time;

Everything sprouting

Back to life,

To cut down

The miseries of time.

The process

Fires on and on

On the silvery screen;

Goes on and on

On the earthly green;

Carries on and on

On the mortal beings;

But un-noticed

Since,

It is the way.

This story does not lay down the principles of living, but it is a story intertwined with many laces. The laces have been connected so perfectly that even if the laces are joined at various places; they seem to be one. That is the beauty of nature that has been created for us.

There are various kinds of lessons in the entire story, but it is unnecessary that everybody learns and follows them. **This story is an attempt at bringing out anomalies in the modern system of living and rectifying them.**

This is a story, a self-help book, a book that is connected and integrated with modern management thoughts.

It's a story made to unravel the roots of the value systems which can help rectify various ailments of modern-day living.

The contents of the book in no way represent any individual or groups, and the characters mentioned are coincidental. There are attempts to search for solutions, and if there are any solutions, it doesn't have to be the only one. There might be better ways to think and look at, and it is on the people of this world to think about the betterment of the future of the earth in every way.

Last, I would like to thank the fishes in my fishbowl and my family for being there while I penned this book. It has been a fantastic three-month journey of writing this book, and I am grateful for being able to write it.

Your journey to self-revelation has just begun.

~ **Neeraj Singhvi**
Author, Life Transformation Coach, Entrepreneur &
Marketing Strategist

TEMPLE
OF
DESTINY

THE BEGINNING OF THE END

1

A bombshell was about to explode inside the deep crevices of his mind. His subconscious mind told him his world, which was till now filled with so much leisure, pleasure, scientific theories, politics and a host of other modern issues, was going to change. Some oblivious forces were pulling him into the deepest zones, not experienced by him before.

Harrod was looking at his leather-covered diary which he had just purchased, because of an impulse that told him he must jot down whatever he would learn in the next few days. He flipped over to the first page and wrote his name. He then flipped to the next page and jotted his first thoughts on this personal diary while travelling to the abode of Guruji.

<u>The Future Beholds</u>

My mind stings me;

What have I done?

What am I doing?

For the same,

What am I going to do?

The pendulum swings

From one end to another;

The petty days

Pass into,

An unending horizon;

All seems to move,

Except me.

For what?

For whom?

Should I move!

None to rejoice

At my happiness,

None to weep

At my sorrows,

Except me!

The time of a lifetime,

Faces me.

Again,

The question puzzles me.

I am helpless,

The decision is useless.

The world is a pleasure,

Yet,

There are loopholes;

I need someone,

A support

For a lifetime.

At the ashram, Guru Satyanand sat in the middle of the hall in an upright posture with his eyes closed. He sat cross-legged in the lotus posture and adorned a pearl white turban on his head with similar coloured white robes on his body. He had three horizontal sandalwood stripes on his forehead which gave him a very spiritual look. The sandalwood stripes were to keep his head cool.

The hall was square measuring approximately two thousand square feet, having brilliant shining white marble flooring and pearly white walls. Small intricate carvings festooned the walls and ceiling of the room. Guruji as everyone called him sat at the centre of it. A very thin ray of light came streaming from the small glass ceiling created in the centre of the hall and diagonally above where he was sitting. It seemed as though a Halo had formed behind him and it felt God-like. There was a stunning silence in the hall and Guruji chanted his mantras on a stable note. The mantras reverberated in the hall in a cascading form. Each word sounded as though a million atoms were striking and bouncing back from the walls, to the place where Guruji sat. Guruji's rhythmic breath before and after each mantra was calculated and someone from the other world seemed to hear them perfectly.

The whole atmosphere was divine.

Some distance away from where Guruji (Guru Satyanand) sat, a glass fishbowl was placed on a raised glass stool, supported by four thin wooden legs. The fishbowl had four goldfishes, two black ones and some green water plants in it. The water was pure, crystal clear and the glass bowl shone resplendently in its purity. While Guruji prayed, the fish swam and played together, unaware of the chants of the great Guru.

Harrod sat in front of Guruji watching him and wanting to understand the deeper meanings of life which he was unaware till now. He had come to Guruji for getting his blessings and to understand the purpose of existence, co-existence and beyond.

THE SIMPLE WAY TO OBSERVE

2

Harrod had come to India from the U.S., after doing a lot of research into the different aspects of life, but still could not understand the purpose of his existence in this world.

Harrod was an educated person. He was a bio-engineer, and science was a part of his everyday life. Although he believed scientific reasons were the basis for every activity, he did not know why life existed at all. This was beyond his comprehension.

Harrod's Indian friend Sam, who had once been to India, had briefed him about Guruji, but internet search results did not yield any leads to Guruji's profound learning. But somehow Harrod's conscience was steadily guiding him and making him feel almost certain that there lay the answers to his questions and also to his future missions.

Immediately after getting briefed about Guruji, Harrod had written a letter to him. Sam had also told him that Guruji's acceptance methods were strange and therefore, acceptance as his disciple was very tough. Guruji knew whom he was supposed to impart his knowledge to and who was supposed to learn from him. His friend had also told him that, although Guruji's methods were strange, he was a soft person and very much contented with what he had. Further, Sam also told him he had heard about Guruji having the blessings of God himself.

In the letter, Harrod had written to Guruji:

"Guruji,

My heartfelt respect for you.

I do not know whether these are the right words, but I somehow sense now that the answers that I am looking for lie with you. My friend from India spoke to me and told me a lot about you. He praised your help for people in need and how you had almost all answers to life's unending ethos and problems.

Sincerely, I have become tired of moving around and sometimes life seems so unsure. There's no direction, there's no comfort zone, and I feel I am moving around aimlessly, even though I have all the comforts of this world.

Sometimes I have felt that life has a lot of other things in store for me and the work that I am doing is just something to make me move forward, but when I get to think about it, there is a feeling that there will be some different turns and twists which are going to shape my life.

Guruji, I have never been in touch with Godmen, although I have heard many people on television proclaiming to be

*one, and somehow, I do not believe humans can be a God.
Yet when people proclaim the same, sometimes it makes
my mind think and recognize them as one. Still, I have not
given in to anyone till now.*

*I have never heard about you, but deep inside my heart, I
have felt that you are the correct person to be with. You
have not advertised yourself and so I could not find
anything about you on the internet. But what I have learnt
from my friend, my conscience seems to accept and I am
therefore writing to you today.*

*Guruji, I would like to be your disciple and would be
happy if you could accept me as one. I am willing to
undergo any kind of task for becoming one of you.*

With regards

Harrod"

Within a few days of his letter, he received a reply from
Guruji.

*"Harrod, you must come here at once, I am waiting for
you."*

It thrilled Harrod to get the one-liner letter from Guruji.
He packed up his knapsack in a hurry and left for India
within a week of receiving Guruji's letter. He quickly
called his friend, Sam, who had referred Guruji to him,
about getting a reply from Guruji so quickly and thanking
him for it.

Guruji was waiting for him near the foothills of the famous Himalayan Mountains in his ashram at Uttarakhand.

In the early hours of the morning when Harrod reached the ashram (religious retreat) or the abode of Guruji, he was told by the ashram's disciples that Guruji would be busy with his meditation and mantra recitation for two hours starting at six a.m. and he could only meet him after that. After a comfortable slumber that night, Harrod had risen early in the morning and was waiting anxiously to meet Guruji. Every moment seemed exciting, as though he was about to learn the absolute truth the same day, as though he would overcome all his mental troubles on this day itself.

At the stroke of eight a.m., Guruji opened his eyes slowly. One of his disciples came in and gave him a glass of warm water. There was still a marked silence in the room. Finally, Guruji spoke. He asked his disciple about Harrod and was told that Harrod was anxiously waiting for him outside. Guruji asked the disciple to bring him in.

As the disciple ushered Harrod into the room, the huge hand-crafted, polished wooden hall gate opened. The gate itself was quite impressive with minute carvings on it. As he entered, Harrod sensed a million strokes of light in every colour gliding into the hall. The light seemed to guide Harrod to where Guruji was sitting. Harrod was in awe and disbelief. He had never imagined that things which he thought we could only create graphically on computers, actually existed with such finesse on earth–an atmosphere that had the masterstroke of God as a painter.

Harrod stepped in slowly and greeted Guruji with folded hands, just like the others would do. Guruji asked Harrod to sit next to him in the same posture as himself. Guruji knew Harrod's purpose in meeting him.

Guruji asked one of his disciples to bring some warm water for Harrod and then asked him about his journey to India. As Harrod narrated, Guruji could feel Harrod's excitement of being there with him. Harrod's pulse was racing faster than the processing speed of the fastest computer on the planet. But Guruji said nothing about it. Patiently, he asked Harrod to wash up and take something for his breakfast from the ashram kitchen. He told Harrod to come and meet him at five in the evening inside the temple.

On Guruji's instructions, one disciple showed Harrod his cottage, his place of bathing, and then when Harrod had taken his bath, the disciple showed him the area where all the disciples ate their food. He also told Harrod about their regular timings for breakfast, lunch and dinner and how the ashram was strict about maintaining them. The timings were set strictly, breakfast at eight in the morning, lunch at one in the noon and dinner at six in the evening-just before sunset.

After his breakfast, Harrod wandered around the ashram, then took his lunch and an afternoon nap as there was nothing else to do. In his mind, Harrod was waiting for the clock to strike five in the evening when he could again meet Guruji and learn the secrets of life from him.

As per the instructions, Harrod reached the temple at the right time, and Guruji made him sit beside him. Once Harrod had taken his seat, Guruji asked him to look around the room where he sat and experience and sense the simplicity and serenity around him. Guruji asked him to look around in minute details and let him know his observations. Guruji's voice was deep, yet calm, and it seemed to come straight from his heart. It was very soothing.

For the next one-hour, Harrod sat with folded legs in the lotus posture. He looked at the front, back, sides and the ceiling of the temple. He did not know why Guruji had asked him to do this. But he dared not question Guruji on his first day at the ashram.

By that time, Guruji had left for the garden, which was just outside the temple gate. Guruji would come back in an hour and would then inquire about Harrod's observations. This was like Harrod's first major examination at the ashram, but he felt thrilled that it was a simple one. One which was only related to observations.

Harrod kept looking around at the temple walls but could figure nothing in the hall except a fishbowl on the raised stool. The room was pure white, yes, but was blank with very delicate carvings on its walls. Everything was so simple, unlike the coloured world outside that he was so used to. To him, the world would be nothing if there were no colours, especially in his home country, where one cannot find anything without colours. Everything in the hall seemed in perfect harmony, including the white colour. He kept sitting impatiently and wanted to just walk off, as he could find nothing significant inside the hall. But he was also sure that Guruji had not asked him to sit there aimlessly without a proper purpose. Although his legs ached while sitting upright in the posture, the thought of getting enlightened kept him waiting there for the next hour.

Finally, after an hour, Guruji walked in. Harrod could see why people revered him. Everything about him was so simple, so realistic and yet so divine.

Guruji came up to Harrod and asked him what he had observed. As Harrod had observed nothing unusual, he replied, "I see the enormous hall, the pure white walls with some very good intricate carvings, the shining white marble flooring, a beautifully carved wooden gate and the fishbowl with six fishes swimming in it".

What is so unusual about the hall? asked Guruji.

"Quite nothing", replied Harrod. It's just so simple and the hall looks great in this white hue.

Guruji came near Harrod and said, "There is a lot to learn from this hall, my son, and you will have to have a lot of patience and endurance for understanding the rules and learning what life has laid out for us. Bring your power of observation above the platform of commoners and look beyond the normal. You must learn to read between the lines which God has so skilfully written for us. From tomorrow your teachings will start and today you can just move around the ashram and get to know everyone here. At five a.m. tomorrow, you must come here and meet me again. One more important thing before we disperse. This place is called the "**Temple of Destiny**"." Guruji left with these words.

It perplexed Harrod. Why did Guruji say, "This place is called the Temple of Destiny"? There was nothing in this hall that had anything to do with Destiny. It was such a simple white hall. What was so special about the hall that Guruji knew, but Harrod could not understand? Harrod would have to wait for another day to learn the truth from Guruji.

THE CYCLES OF SELF REFINEMENT

3

On the next day, since he was quite impatient to meet Guruji, Harrod woke up early at 4 a.m. He washed his face, went to the toilet, freshened up and wore his usual blue jeans and a white t-shirt with some strokes of coloured images on it and went to meet Guruji.

As Harrod walked up to the temple, Guruji directed one of his disciples to get Harrod to change his clothes into a pure white one like the one the others were wearing. They ushered Harrod into another room where he changed into white cotton robes, as instructed. The clothes were quite awkward for Harrod, as this was the first time, he was wearing anything like this. It was a traditional Indian outfit for saints, and all the disciples were wearing a similar type of covering. As soon as Harrod had changed, he instantly felt a part of all of them.

After changing his clothes, Harrod came back to the temple and sat next to Guruji.

After asking him to sit in the lotus-like, cross-legged posture, Guruji asked Harrod to chant some mantras along with him. The sound of AUM reverberated once again in the room. The mantras were plain words with no meaning for Harrod, but Harrod had to repeat them after Guruji. Harrod found amazing energy run down his body whenever he repeated the mantras after Guruji. 10 minutes of chanting the same words seemed like an eternity to Harrod and then Guruji finally spoke, "Harrod, you come from a faraway land - A land having a different culture, thought process and mindset. Also, you have a religion that you respect and which helps and guides you to your goal. Here in this ashram, we do not preach religion, we preach life because religion is man-made while life is a creation of nature. If there is life, only then, will there be a religion. I want you to understand the power of Mother Nature, the power which has brought life into Mother Nature, and the power to understand Mother Nature itself. Without Mother Nature, we would be nothing, nothing at all. Nature rises above all religions, above all caste, creed and race. Time rules it and we, the living beings, are just the support which nature needs to recreate itself, repeatedly".

Guruji continued, "Harrod, yesterday when I asked you to observe this temple internally, you could not understand the reason for this room's existence. This place, as I have named it, is called the "**Temple of Destiny**", and in time to come, you will understand why. But first, let me tell you about this room and why we call it a temple. You have observed very well that everything about the room is simple, white and serene. But when you close the doors of the room, it becomes pitch dark inside and the only light is the thin ray of light percolating from above, through the glass panes. This room is a replica of the universe. When closed, it is dark, just like the universe and the light that you see acts like the sun. In the dark space, there is a fishbowl at the centre of the room with a few live fishes.

The bowl represents the earth and just as the earth is two-thirds water, so is the bowl filled with two-thirds water and the fishes and plants depict life on this earth. At all sides there is darkness, but this faint light makes us see the bowl, just as the earth is visible as the only planet with life on it, from a distance. The stand, on which the bowl rests, is there just to act as a support for the bowl to keep itself in its orbit and if the bowl just moves a bit, it will crash bringing life in it to a halt. But when this very room is opened, it throws up immense opportunities to think about. Everything becomes so bright and breathable. You can breathe a fresh bout of air and can think about various things which you could do with this room, just as the sunlight guides you to explore a lot of things on this earth and universe".

He then said, "Harrod, do you now understand why I had asked you to observe this room? Your classes will start in the coming morning. But before your classes start, let me tell you how you will proceed with your curriculum to learn what you are destined to, and what you are here for.

Harrod, during the entire course with me, you will undergo four cycles.

> ➤ *The Cycle of Connectivity and Integration*

> ➤ *The Cycle of Wisdom*

> ➤ *The Cycle of Self Recognition*

> ➤ *The Cycle of Self Actualization*

These cycles will be the basis of your education, just as they have become the basis of a few others as well. When you learn these and get through, you will reach millions of people and teach them about the greatness of life that you will have learnt here. These cycles will help you in reaching beyond yourself and will help you in understanding the purpose of being here on this planet.

During the first cycle of Connectivity and Integration, you will learn to understand the reason we all are connected and how we all integrate. You will also realize the power of concentration during this time and how it helps in bringing a balance.

During the cycle of Wisdom, you will travel to different places and get to learn the wisdom which wise people have left us with. In this phase, you will gain wisdom on why we need to learn the ways of the world and to master the reasons they have made things the way they are.

During the cycle of Self Recognition, you will learn how to understand yourself. You will learn why you are here and what makes up you.

During the cycle of Self Actualization, you will attain the powers which you have never comprehended and which will help you carry forward the teachings that you will learn here with me.

But the first cycle first and you cannot hop on to different cycles without completing the one before it. Some cycles can be of short duration and some longer, but each cycle will take you to a different level and each cycle will help you gain insights into different aspects of life. Each cycle will be more difficult than the other, but if you want to achieve success, then you must go through all the cycles with proper concentration and energy. If you leave midway, whatever you have learnt during the last cycle will be wiped out of your mind and then you will return to your old ways of living life. But, I know, you are here to learn and you will.

Your teaching will start tomorrow with the first cycle of Connectivity and Integration, which is the most important cycle for getting through to the last.

At 5 a.m. you must come to the temple after taking your bath, chant the AUM mantra for ten minutes as I will teach you and then sit next to the fishbowl for an hour observing it minutely.

Within AUM lies the beginning and the end of everything in this world, and therefore this mantra is very important in everyone's life. The AUM mantra must be recited in this fashion–

'aaaaaaooooooooooooommmmm'.

Listen to the pitch in the word and the chanting with mouth closed at the ending letters 'mmmmmmm'. The "aaaaaa" sound seems to come from just below our navel, the "ooooo" sound seems to come from the centre of the chest just below the sternum, while the "mmmm" seems to come from the centre of the neck just between the two collarbones and the sound ends in the mouth on the lips. This mantra takes care of activating our chakras in our body, which governs our body systems. The entire pronunciation is very important for the chanting to be effective. What is also important is the inhaling and exhaling of your breath during this chant as these controls the internal systems of your body and help AUM achieve its aim? Be slow and steady in your recitation, and each one must be recited clearly. The AUM mantra will help you learn the power of concentration and the power of Connectivity and Integration. As the days pass by, the duration of this mantra recitation will increase and ten minutes will then increase to one hour and then to two hours subsequently. This is because the power of concentration will develop only when the period of chanting increases and the irrelevant thoughts that rule your mind from time to time is thrown away into the recycle bin. Learn to think through the blank space and time with no pre-occupied thoughts."

When Guruji spoke, there was complete silence. There was no one else to comment, and there were no suggestions from anyone. Everyone knew whatever Guruji stated was the way to attain the goal, which was destined for them. Guruji was supreme, Guruji was the learned one. He had the powers to teach, and he had the reasons for it. There were no questions when he taught, as he would provide reasons for everything he said.

Guruji continued to speak to Harrod, "After the chanting of the AUM mantra, every day you must make one observation from the bowl, the fishes, the plants and its surroundings and then let me know about your observation that very day at 5 p.m. So, every day, your day will start at 5 a.m. and at 5 p.m. you must meet me and discuss your observations. If you have understood its meaning, let me know. If not, then I will explain the significance of the observation to you. You will keep on learning till you understand the complete significance of the "**Temple of Destiny**"."

Harrod was quite amazed at what he had just heard. He had learnt one thing that day - to think simple, above the scientific principles and the various theories that he had once learnt when he was studying in college. In simplicity lay the knowledge. All the knowledge which he gathered till then, had to be kept on backstage. The front stage of life would be the ashram where he would start his new studies, with Guruji playing the lead role as a teacher.

Harrod was 30 years old and had the experience of working in science laboratories after completing a master's degree. He had been involved with many scientists and bio-science discoveries in reputed laboratories around the world. He had learnt to debate scientific experiments, to reason out various theories, but was still not satisfied with what he was doing or what he had accomplished. So, here he was with Guruji, trying to learn things beyond the realms of science which he was once involved with and with whom he lived and shared his life.

Something was so special about Guruji, that it pulled Harrod closer to him just like the pull of the iron nail next to a magnet. The iron nail will get attracted to the magnet and, after sticking together for some time, would start inheriting some properties of the magnet itself. Of course, it would not guarantee a complete takeover of the magnetic pull, but inheritance itself would help it attract similar iron pellets with a similar force.

So here was Harrod, attracted and attached to Guruji, and the longer he would be with him, the better he would understand the reason for his coming there and get to imbibe the knowledge that Guruji would impart to him. The magnet would do its trick only when Harrod kept himself near it. Somehow, this aspect became quite clear to Harrod and he would do anything to continue to be a part of this important phase of his life.

Harrod went to his cottage and slept there with his mind wandering over a lot of different thoughts.

During the past few days, even though, Harrod's focus was the teachings of Guruji to enable him to learn about his life's purpose, today there were digressing thoughts in his mind asking him, whether his decision of coming to India in search of his answers, was correct. But being tired by now, he dozed off with a multitude of thoughts in his mind.

CYCLE

OF

CONNECTIVITY

AND INTEGRATION

THE FIRST CYCLE BEGINS

4

Guruji's enlightened teaching on the first day had begun. Harrod obediently got up early in the morning, washed up and went to the temple where his first teachings were about to be unravelled. At 5 a.m. he reached the temple and as per Guruji's instruction, for the next 10 minutes got himself engrossed in chanting the AUM mantra. As soon as this got over, he got himself another stool for sitting and observing the fishbowl.

Harrod sat on the stool which was like the one where the bowl with the fishes rested. He looked into the fishbowl for the first time with a lot of interest and wanted to understand what Guruji wanted to teach him. He was in a rush to learn everything instantly.

In the beginning, he saw four goldfishes & two black fishes swimming in the bowl. The glass bowl was transparent and two-thirds of it was filled with water. He could not understand what Guruji wanted him to know from these innocent-looking fishes. The fishes were alive, lively and looked beautiful in the fishbowl, especially when placed in the pure white room. The colourful fishes looked vibrant in the white surrounding. The front door of the temple was open and the outside light streamed inside. The sun was just waking up. Everything was so fresh. But Harrod could understand nothing after observing the fishes on the first day, apart from the fact that these were small and beautiful creatures and just like Guruji had explained, they represented the living beings on the earth. Yes, they were living, but what about it? What was Guruji trying to make him learn through the medium of the fishes? This thought only made him think deeper about what Guruji was going to teach him.

Harrod continued to look into the bowl, just like Guruji had asked him to do. The fishes kept playing, and he watched them with great interest, just as if a small boy would have watched them with much interest for the first time. After watching them for over half an hour, he got tired and since he was not getting any kind of message from the fishes; he quit watching for the time being. He knew Guruji was very knowledgeable and therefore must have asked Harrod to observe the fishbowl with a definite purpose. Another half an hour passed by with no result, and since now his time was over, he left the temple with no story. The temple would now get occupied by the other devotees and disciples of Guruji for the morning prayers.

The entire day passed and Harrod was quite eager to ask Guruji about what he could learn from the fishes. He had his morning breakfast and then his lunch and then slept for a while. But his sleep was time-bound, and he was getting disturbed again and again by the thought of getting his first insight by Guruji. What was Guruji going to reveal to him?

In the evening, when the clock struck five, just as Guruji had promised, they called Harrod to the ashram garden. He approached Guruji, paid his respects with folded hands by bending his head in front of Guruji. Guruji reciprocated and then asked him, "Harrod, what did you notice today".

Harrod recalled, "Guruji, I did everything like you had asked, but could not get to know what the glass bowl with the fishes could teach me. I tried to observe, but the only thing that I got to know was that the fishes looked beautiful in the bowl, they were of different colours and they swam in the water-filled in the bowl like any other fish would have done".

Guruji smiled faintly and then said, "Harrod, you need to learn a lot. The first thing is maintaining our timelines. It is an important aspect of our lives. Just as I had asked you, you had done everything on time, which is very good. The essence of time is very important, and if you follow your time concerning your work, you will know how to manage it properly. Throughout the day, you had maintained your time to getting up, washing up, eating your food and now meeting me. We must respect time at every stage or else one fine day we will find that we have used up all our time in this life doing nothing worthwhile and will repent for that and beg God for more time than allotted to us in this lifetime. Time Management is the need of the hour and once you respect it, you find that time will also start respecting your hard work. Our lives are connected by strings of time, and each second is precious and is calculated by divine forces.

This has been explained by nature itself. The Earth revolves and rotates within particular time zones. Days and nights come and go in regular time frames. The moon rotates within a particular time. The other planets also follow their designated paths and time frames. Everything in the universe has a fixed time. Even when you observe our body systems, you will find this aspect to be very true. Babies take nine months to come into shape before entering this world. They crawl after a fixed number of months and start walking after a fixed period. Biologically, we all sleep during the night and work during the day, which is also controlled by time. If you were to observe correctly, you find that those people, who exercise regularly, live a better and healthier life. Better life here means a much healthier life in terms of body and mind. A lot of them will tell you that living a better life means wearing costly clothes, living in big houses, wearing expensive jewellery, etc. But this is only living a materialistic life, which has been created and invented by us. It is not a gift of nature to all of us. This is short and momentary happiness and in the long term will only harm us. All these people who lead a materialistic life will realize this when their end time is near and what they can take with them at the end of the journey is just their inner happiness and nothing else. Nature will help them learn this aspect when the correct time comes. Even in this, there is a time and we all have a span. We take birth and according to our own time; we die. Thus, the importance of time. Time controls us and we just have to use it in the best possible manner to achieve our ends."

"Secondly", Guruji continued, "Harrod, I had asked you to observe the fishbowl and tell me about your first observation, but your mind has been occupied by the thought of the literal meaning of the question that I had asked, rather than the observation itself. Of course, you are free to think about anything in this world, but here, if you want to learn, you must do only what is told. You have done, what was told but the thought behind it was being greedy, of being expectant. You thought you could learn everything on the first day of your life here, which is not possible. A man takes an entire life to learn, yet cannot complete his desire to do so. But continuous and sustained training to the brain can help one, gain knowledge beyond the common boundaries of humanity. Your thought process was wrong. You were thinking of killing the hen to get all the golden eggs at once. The hen will die and you will get nothing from it. Therefore, the essence here is that we must learn to respect our inner thought–our conscience–our subconscious mind, which you and I have. Every human being has it, and so do you. Try to listen to it. If you respect your inner thoughts, your outward thoughts, which you use externally the most, will respect you and help you learn the truth."

How could Guruji get to know so much about his inner thoughts? Harrod was trying to reason out but was not being able to comprehend.

"Thirdly, Harrod," Guruji said, "You must learn to respect the value of patience. You thought you would learn everything in an hour. This is not possible, even though you must have heard people say, "impossible is the adjective of fools". You must understand that patience is not a science, but a value within you. You must give time to patience if you want to learn the inner secrets of life.

Let me tell you a simple story. There was once a beggar who lived his life begging on the streets. He had a family of four to feed. His wife and two children stayed on one pavement, inside a house built with paper and plastic bags gathered from the streets. Even when he had to feed everybody, including himself, he tried to save money from the money he earned every day. He used to keep part of his earnings under the cloth where he slept.

One day, his wife asked him to count all his savings. On counting, it amazed him to learn, he had saved nearly twenty thousand rupees. Although his wife insisted upon spending a part of this on some of their daily needs, he took the money and put it into a bank. He came to know from his friends that this sum would keep on growing through interest if he kept it in the bank.

In time to come, the beggar grew old, and his children grew into adults. One day, he asked his children to check his account in the bank. It was nearly thirty years and all these thirty years; he would save and deposit into his bank. Little by little, his fortune had grown from twenty thousand to a million.

The beggar was happy that his patience had now borne fruit and his family could now enjoy a life which he could only dream of.

Harrod, patience will ultimately pay. If the beggar would have lost his patience, he would have spent everything he had earned and could end up with his family begging for another lifetime. But his patience, wit and endurance made him save so much that his old age would now be happier and his children would not have to beg anymore. They could lead a better life.

So have patience, and you will only learn more and more each time. Don't jump to conclusions. Keep doing your work diligently and the fruits will be sweeter than you can ever think.

Harrod, it is already two hours since I met you today. Even if you have not known, today, the fishbowl has taught you three important aspects and values of life: *time, concentration and patience*. Every day, before you go to sleep, you must note down whatever you have learnt during the day. You must give yourself half an hour before you go to sleep and recollect everything that has transpired during the day. It will give you a tool to act upon, for your next day. It is not a record of events, but a recollection of things that have gone through to act more positively on a coming day. You may destroy it if you feel like, in time to come."

Guruji continued, "Harrod, today your time to part from me has come. I have other important matters to attend to. Tomorrow, you must once again repeat what you observed today. This time observe well and tell me whatever you see without looking at the consequence or the imagining the result of it." Guruji left him with these words.

Harrod was quite amazed at his first day's teachings. He could never think that without reading or any explanations, he could learn so much about life's values. How simply Guruji had converted his work during the day into a respectful thought process.

He walked up to his room, sat there for a few minutes, still dazed by Guruji's thoughts. He then took his dinner at 7 p.m. The dinner comprised yellow lentil curry, vegetable curry and a few chapattis (wheat bread). This was his second dinner at the ashram. He was not used to this kind of food but liked it as it was quite simple. He had no choice. After dinner, he wrote whatever he was told that day by Guruji. It took him an hour to recall and jot down everything in his leather diary. During his college days and his professional working days, he had been a perfect listener, and that is how he got good grades everywhere. But here at the ashram, the grades were different. Here the grades were on his life and not on his lifestyle. Here the grades on life's values and not the value of money. What he would learn here would decide his life's career and his career, he knew, for the moment lay in Guruji's hands.

He went off to sleep early with the thought of getting up early the next morning and observing the fishes once again on the next day.

MEDIUM OF CONNECTIVITY

5

Not being used to getting up early, it was a difficult proposition for Harrod to jump out of his cot laid on the floor. But Harrod made the effort and got up early with the help of his alarm clock. He quickly washed up and went out of his room. As he was a bit early, he had the chance of watching one disciple clean the pathway that led to the temple. The disciple wore white clothes as per the temple guidelines and had a broom in his hands. Dried leaves and dust were strewn along the temple pathway. The disciple would clear the pathway by collecting the dried leaves in a bag. This activity lasted for some 20 minutes till they cleared the entire path. The disciple then went and collected water in a wooden bucket and washed the entire path by spraying the water from the bucket with his hands. After watching him for some time, Harrod walked up to the temple.

He sat down with folded legs in the lotus position, his two wrists on his knees and his thumb and forefinger joined outside with the other three fingers stretched outside his palm. Guruji explained the posture to him on the first day itself, and Harrod learnt it better by watching other disciples doing the same during his first day at the ashram.

He then chanted AUM for ten minutes, before resuming his observation of the fishbowl.

Once again, he watched the fishbowl with the fishes swimming in it and the water unmoved by their movement inside it. But this time he was not thinking about the thought of gathering any lessons from it immediately. He was only trying to observe what was happening in the fishbowl. His observation was sharp, nevertheless, after watching the fishbowl for an hour, he could not gather any significant inference except that the fishes were swimming happily, the plants swayed and the water was calm.

That evening at 5 p.m. he met Guruji and told him about his observation. He knew there was nothing exceptional in his observations, and Guruji would agree to it.

But, on hearing, Guruji explained, "Harrod, today you have made a certain positive observation. You have watched the fishes, the water, the bowl and the plants with the focus that you were supposed to. Have you noticed something new there? Have you wondered, what was so common between the water, plant and fishes, that we have put together and how they are now living in a place from where they could watch the world outside, listen to the chants, the music and people talking"?

Harrods thoughts suddenly seemed to sway. He knew now that there was some purpose in his observation, which he could not perceive, but what was it? He was yearning to learn more.

Guruji explained, "Harrod, you are the common medium of all the four things that you have observed. You were destined to meet these six fishes and derive certain outcomes from them. Just as you were destined to meet me and being accepted as my disciple. These fishes do not know that they will live in that bowl, just as you have neither imagined that you would come into this world and meet me one day.

The plants, water and the fishbowl help the fishes in their day to day living. So is the case with you. You live on this planet with the help of earth, water, oxygen and sunlight. You must have learnt during your science classes in school, the plants help in the circulation of oxygen and carbon dioxide and thus help in maintaining a balance of atmospheric changes around the world. The plants are integral to this world, just as you or any other living matter is. The water is the medium that helps the fishes and plants stay alive. Without this, the fishes would have died long ago or probably would never have existed.

The bowl is the medium where the fishes will live just as we all live on this planet, and water is the primary medium that helps us all exist on this planet. Without water, we would all be non-existent. Water makes up two-thirds of the earth, and so does the human body and all other living organisms on this planet. We are all made up of water and it will consume us, eventually. Water is the reason for our birth; it is the healer, the destroyer, and the ultimate consumer.

Similarly, the sun is a life-giver. There are rays in the sun which are integral in the process of life and it helps life germinate. But again, the sun depends on the water on this planet to create plants and living things, which help in providing life on this planet. You will have noticed that the fishes will die if there is no water, but without sunlight, they could still exist, but in a unique environment.

That is why they have all come together. These fishes were destined to be placed in this Temple and be a part of my teachings to you. All the four things that you have observed today, have been destined to listen to the everyday mantras and chants of the temple devotees, and they are also exposed to the care of the same people. That is why they are here together.

You will also notice, after some time the water will be required to be changed in the bowl, the plants are required to be changed if they get rotten or damaged, but the glass bowl will not get changed until and unless it is broken and the fishes will always be there till their final breath or till there is water or their life span has not ended.

Similarly, you and I are also a part of this magnificent creation where the earth will not get destroyed till we do not damage its natural life instincts. Humanity will also remain so long as the earth is there, but the plants will get replaced on brief notice and the water will be changed for purification through a natural process. Living things on this planet will continue to evolve till we do something which will help destroy its future. We maintain the earth's natural habitat.

Just as there was some special reason for you to come to me, there is reason in everything that occurs on this planet. Some feel it is scientific, others feel it is because of the divine power, but in actuality, it is the mix of both. Divine interventions have created science, and we are just living science and not divine intervention principles. Understanding these principles is important if we want to understand our science and its existence.

There is a reason in everything that has been created. The earth is round and so are the other planets and so are its trajectories. The universe is a vast expanse but we do not know its shape, but who knows that it might be an enormous ball itself within which we are all revolving and rotating. We have to understand why life is only there on Earth in the entire solar system and not there on any other planet. There are reasons for that too."

With this said, Guruji left Harrod for the day. Harrod had not in his wildest dreams comprehended any such inference from his observation. But he was getting to know everything he was doing and everything which he saw or heard or felt, had a purpose and it was up to him to recognize and learn from it. From now on, a new chapter had opened in his life. He would watch every step that he would take and every time he took one, he would think about the purpose behind the same.

That evening, after having his dinner, he wrote everything in his notebook. But he was dumbstruck by what Guruji had told him. Harrod had known the scientific principles of life but had never really thought that there is a power beyond science, which is creating and moulding science itself. He had been praying to God. He knew God could do strange things, but he had never thought that this power whom he worshipped as God, had created a wonder-struck universe, designed it in such perfect and beautiful unison. This beauty was beyond the beauty that he had seen in his everyday adventurous life.

The more he thought about what Guruji had explained that day, the more he would get deeply involved within his inner self. Harrod was now getting deeply engrossed in life within himself, and yet he was unaware of this. The more he thought, the more he wrote, and this carried on till all his thoughts got over.

Different thoughts engulfed Harrod. Before he visited the ashram, Harrod had read about ghastly explosions rocking cities and towns in different parts of the world. This thought kept on disturbing him. So, while he was feeling sleepy, he also kept writing and in his half-sleep he scribbled:

The Unknown

The object rolled,

Slowly and stealthily,

Into the pandemonium-

Of the open market,

Escaping the local eye.

And then!

A sudden explosion,

Marked the place

In total silence.

The brutal attacked,

The rulers informed,

But the innocent

Suffered the loss.

He felt tired after writing the notes and as he wrote the last line; he went off to sleep with the pen still in his hand and his diary lying next to him.

COLOUR YOUR LIFE

6

The next morning Harrod got up on time and realized the pen and diary were still lying next to him. He kept them aside and went to wash up.

He was more than eager to go back to the temple to learn more from Guruji. Just as he had seen the disciple clean the pathway the day earlier, he saw another disciple clearing the dust and then cleaning the pathway with water. Harrod did not know whether every disciple had to do these things or that there were just a few who were assigned these kinds of tasks. Was Harrod also going to be given such a job? What would this teach him?

Harrod had seen cleaning on the streets in his hometown as well. His city was kept clean in the same way, but with the help of modern mechanized and automated tools.

But, as per Guruji's instructions, Harrod now had to take care of his morning job only, that is, his chanting and observation of the bowl. He knew he had to reach the temple on time and complete the job given to him by Guruji. He had already started respecting Guruji a lot after hearing him for the past few days.

He reached the temple exactly on time and got on his assigned work. After chanting the AUM mantra, his observation for the day began. In the light of what he had been told the previous day, he sat down to watch the fishbowl again. After an hour he finished and walked out of the temple and was glad that he had made another observation.

During the day and till after lunch, Harrod's mind kept him intriguing on the morning incident of watching the disciple cleaning the pathway. He didn't know why the thought stuck to his mind. Thinking about all this, he went off to sleep. 20 minutes later, he suddenly got up as if an answer had struck him and he jotted down his thoughts in his diary.

Day's Incipient

The morning light became bright

After the moonlit night.

The birds started chirping,

In the early hours of the morning.

The fresh-looking nature

Looked still fresher,

When the cool morning zephyr

Touched nature's natural beauty.

And then, the flowers bloomed

As one streak of light

Hits its feathered petals.

The disappearing somnolence

Of the people

Marked the day's massive work.

But as all these happened,

The owl,

Took to hiding

After the night's fitful fever.

And the watchman

After his nightly errands,

Still tapping his mighty broomstick

Went home to sleep,

Leaving the surrounding streets

To be happily looked after

By the hustle & bustle of,

The day's bursting crowds.

Having penned his thoughts over the morning events, he was happy that the recurring thought had been translated into something more special. He was getting to understand the meaning of nature, more than what he had read in the books. He was impressed with himself. But he knew this was not the end. Guruji had greater plans for him, a greater vision and much more devoted learning ahead for him. He wanted to show this work to Guruji. But would Guruji look or hear about it? Would it impress Guruji?

Again, that day at 5 p.m. Harrod met Guruji and before he could narrate what he had written about his morning observing, Guruji asked him, "Harrod, what did you observe at the temple today?"

Harrod said, "Guruji, today I observed something different. I watched the wonder of nature. There were two goldfishes with slightly longer tails and two with the normal ones. There were also two black and beautiful small fishes. They all swam as if there were no hindrances in their path. The goldfishes were smarter as they were larger than the black ones. As I was putting the food pills in the bowl, I could see the goldfishes jump on them, while the smaller black ones tried their luck and eventually landed up eating smaller pieces of the pills. That is all that I observed, although it differed slightly from what I had observed earlier".

Harrod didn't know what else to say, so he stayed quiet after this and waited for Guruji to spray his profound wisdom on him.

Finally, Guruji said, "Harrod, you have observed well. First, you have observed the colours of nature - Colours that have provided meaning to nature. Nature is very vibrant and the brilliance shows in its colours. Different species have been blessed with different colours and each one is unique. Nature in its bounty has given us what it recognizes most - beautiful colours.

Have you noticed the bright sunlight? If you were to stand below a rock and watch a fraction of the sunlight strike the rock from above, you will see the sunlight break into vibrant colours which you call VIBGYOR. Can you imagine what the sun comprises and how the light has been produced to provide you with the colours of your life? We have the power to see and so we can look at this phenomenon, but can we create such an extraordinary phenomenon ourselves? Can we recreate the same colours and are we able to put in new colours that nature already does not have in this universe? It is almost impossible for the human species to make anything new which nature has not given. If we have to add one new colour, it will only be possible with the help of the power, which God will bestow upon us.

Look at the strangeness of colours. They shine and provide us with visual extravaganzas. Every colour speaks of different emotions and each colour is relevant for different occasions. Red speaks of rage, Yellow of fire, blue for the ocean and sky, and a mix of these colours creates different colour combinations and relate to different things. They are with us during our happiness, during our celebrations, and with us in our sorrows. They are black in places and white in other places. Where white shows us simplicity, black shows us the dark path through life. Colours make us say "wow" and colours make us discard things. See how colours have so nicely integrated into our lives and those of other living species. Look at how we are connected with these colours and we cannot live without them either. Even people, who cannot see, see the darkness within themselves and imagine colours in the outside world. Without colours, what would our world be? We are nothing without colours.

Second, you have also noticed the beautiful shapes of the fishes which show us that God has provided each of the species a different shape to adapt to its environment. Your body differs from that of a tiger, so is the tiger's body different from a dog and so is the dog's body different from a mouse and so is the mouse different from a lizard and so is the lizard different from a moth and so is the moth different from a bee and so is a bee different from an ant and so is the ant different from the tiny insects and they differ from the various insects that exist but cannot be viewed by us through our naked eye. The list is endless. Each one is different in its form and God has taken care to see that they do not fall into each other's category, but within their clan or group, they remain quite similar. But then again within each clan, no one is quite the same as another, just as you don't resemble me, in terms of body construction, constitution, knowledge, strength and various other factors that God has so magnanimously bestowed upon us.

Just like the colours, the shapes play important roles in our lives. And it is this aspect that helps us in recognizing them. It is the combination of colours and shapes that form their differential basis. Shapes help us adapt to our environments and also help us live. You must have noticed the fishes in the bowl and should have already known that their bodies help them swim efficiently in water, just like the ergonomic shapes of birds help them glide through air extremely well.

Third, you have understood that food is very important for all living things. You saw the fishes jump for the food, as each one did not have the intelligence of knowing whether there was sufficient food for everyone. There was a desire amongst each one to be alive and food being the only source that they know, jumped at it to get it first. I want you to understand why in poverty-stricken countries, people want to snatch food from one another even though some countries provide sufficient food to them. They feel if they have more, they will live more. The food itself has its shelf life, and they are not aware that food gets oxidized in the open and can turn toxic after a certain period. So, it makes more sense to share than to hoard food. The fresher the food, the better it is for our health. The fishes teach us to be more sensible in knowing the secrets of food and to share the food with everyone. It is not just an act of kindness, but an act that can save a lot of lives. Give more than you can take. The supreme power or force will see that you will get, only if you give.

Sharing matters in our lives. The animals are not aware of this, so they snatch. But humans can understand better. We understand the meaning of sharing and caring. Look at children and you will understand this better. We must all learn from children. They are innocent of any pre-taught lessons. If you see two toddlers, you find they will give and take things from each other. But if you see slightly grown-ups, you find they will not want to give away the things they like, as they have been taught in this way. These thoughts grow bigger with time and finally when we do not get the things we want; we want to snatch them away. Toddlers and babies are our best teachers. They teach us about traits that have been provided to us unselfishly by the supreme force and which we have lost on our way to adulthood.

Fourth, you observed that the larger fishes ate their food in abundance and the smaller & weaker fishes could not even fill their stomachs. This aspect teaches us we should protect the weaker, otherwise, they will perish and it will break the balance of the world. Just as there is a necessity for stronger people, there is an equal necessity for the weaker people. Power or strength cannot attain everything. If one were to get anything by sheer power or strength, the same will be short-lived and you will enjoy it only for a brief period. But if you get anything by the willingness of others, you will get it for a lifetime. You must have read about famous Kings, some of whom have been defeated by force and others who had the blessings of their people and lived on for generations. The Kings with the blessings of the people were always likely to survive more than the other kings who lived on just power to achieve their goals. That is why now; countries with democracies are likely to survive much more than others, as in a democracy everything is for the people, of the people and by the people."

"Harrod," Guruji continued, "I will not cite examples, but I will make you learn the truth only. Examples are many, and you could find many along the road of life. The fishes, the bowl, the water and the room are all mediums of expressions and God has bestowed this medium on me to teach others about the truths of life. Once you learn, you are free to take the course you want, but in the end, you must promise me you will also teach others about these truths in whatever way you feel like. This has to be a part of your life's mission."

Harrod promised to do whatever Guruji wanted from him. He was fast becoming Guruji's devout follower. Harrod did not know what life had in store for him after this, but his sixth sense was telling him that whatever it would be, it would be most beneficial for humanity. He was someone who was chosen for the benefit of all humankind.

Guruji had left for the day, leaving Harrod to complete his day's activity and take a rest in the end.

PURPOSE OF LIFE

7

The following morning Harrod got up as usual, and after his early morning chores set for the temple.

Harrod was quite wonder-struck with the fishes that day. The fishes swayed as if their body had no bones, their structure supported the body and they graciously moved their bodies across the clear water. It was the most beautiful moment that Harrod had ever seen. They seemed to be thrilled, and the vigour with which they danced was worth looking at. Every movement comprised a hundred variations, and someone had to take a close look to realize this. While he watched all this, he went deeper into his thought about the life forms and the wilderness in which they all existed. But it was not the case with all the fishes that were swaying in the water. It was just two of the goldfishes who seemed to dance. The other two goldfishes just followed them or sometimes swam their way, while the smaller black fishes played around. Even while playing, the small black fishes were quick with their moves and although their movement was not so gracious, they added the flavour of colour to the whole bowl.

Harrod got some idea of their smooth movements, but he still could not understand the true significance of this new observation he had made. After an hour of watching them this way and finding no other significant thing, he found his time was over and he went back to his cottage.

As usual, during the day, Harrod carried on with his daily routine, but he was not sure of what was happening to him. Something strange was now dragging him along with the help of the fishes. He wanted to know the message that the fishes were trying to deliver to him, but could not decipher. It was a situation where his mind was full of stress, but he still felt that there were answers which he would get and propel him forward.

He waited for Guruji to explain this to him.

As usual, Guruji came to the garden at 5 p.m. and this time Harrod was waiting for him. As Harrod bowed his head with folded hands, Guruji asked, "Harrod, something seems to trouble you today. What is it?"

Harrod explained the morning observation to Guruji and asked, "Guruji what's so special about what I saw and which has been tormenting me throughout the day."

Guruji explained, "I can see your observation of the fishes is growing every day and you are getting closer to them each day. It is a good thing. You are observing and learning new things daily. But you have to learn to get to the inner meaning of whatever you are watching. All humans are subject to this. They all feel that whatever they see or hear is the truth because that is what their senses show them. They cannot understand the deeper meaning of each of the activities. Every activity is pre-determined, and we are just performing our duty without this knowledge. Our mind, body and soul all act in unison for this pre-programmed prophesy. It is only those who realize the significance of the occurrence that can explain to you why the incident happened, after all. Some dislike and fight over it; others accept it, and yet some people want to live with it. You will recognize it as time carries on. That is why I am here, to guide and teach you to recognize this magical fact of life."

"Come with me," Guruji exclaimed. Guruji took Harrod to an open space and Guruji explained, "Harrod, you see this place is open, is free from any bonds, yet there are living things here that are bonded and others like the birds in the sky fly freely. The birds also have their connections with the earth, and so are also bound to it. They can't just keep flying around. They need a place to rest, to lay their eggs, to make a home, which is where their connection with the earth is established."

"But Guruji, that's not only what I observed. As I told you", Harrod jumped. Guruji raised his hand and stopped him. "Harrod", Guruji explained, "you must not jump to immediate conclusions, but understand the true meaning of today's exercise. You must learn to listen, learn patiently, and get to understand the deeper meaning of anything that you observe or act in life. Whatever you do also has an inner meaning which is connected in some form, to the other facts of life. So, the chain of events is established, and each chain is connected to our actions while staying on earth.

See, we are here at this place with a purpose, you to learn from me and me to make you understand and learn. This binds us. We know the reason for being here and we have a purpose. The earth binds the trees, the garden and the small plants, as they can't grow without the earth and water. But the birds, the insects or the smaller animals and reptiles like the snakes or frog do not know the reason for being here. They can't reason and know they should be there with the help of their instincts, that this place is their home and they will find their food here. They walk, fly or run freely with no fear or knowledge of what lies ahead for them.

Just like that, few fishes enjoy the water freely while others just follow and yet others are there because they are destined to be there for some other purpose, which life has determined for them.

Similarly, you saw the movement of the fishes today. You saw the twists and turns of a few of the fishes. It was the most delighting thing for you. You enjoyed every bit. Whenever there are such movements at any place on Earth and when such movements are created by forces created by nature, you find that we all enjoy such things. Even when humans create such movements when they dance or act, we all enjoy it. These movements create euphoria within us, and our brains respond to it in definite and hyper patterns. It feels as if there is enjoyment everywhere on this planet.

Similarly, nature has provided the fishes with this unique ability of swimming while others do not have it. Just like nature has provided you and me with a unique ability of learning and teaching that has not been provided to other species on the planet. It is just that we cannot recognize this till we are made aware of it. Ordinary people use just 5% of the total brainpower that has been given to us. If we were to just use another 5%, then others would think that we are God gifted. Imagine what would happen and what we could do if we used the rest of the 95%. You are also one of the many who use just 5% of your ability and what I want you to do is go up to at least 25% in the next few years and this would help you achieve the purpose that you have been assigned and destined to do. If we could use 100%, we would become the creators and not the users anymore. That is the difference between God and us. God is there in every one of us and we have to just recognize this to move forward.

Coming back to the fishes, nature has provided the ability for the fishes to sway and move around. With the stroke of their fins, they can move with no difficulty through the water. They can cut through the water with little effort, just as the birds cut through the air with no effort. They have been designed in a way that they can adapt to such environments in their special ways. We have to learn from the fishes to cut through the clutter and sway our way through our lives as smoothly as them. There will be difficulties and problems at every step that we take in life, but we have to deal with them with ease and find solutions to every problem that arises. The solutions are there for every problem, but we need to close our eyes, contemplate and find them in peace and we will get them. We have the desire and the ability already inside us but we only need the willingness to sail through, effortlessly.

You will have noticed that while the fishes move around, there is no disturbance to the water in the bowl. Similarly, this is the case with birds. As I told you earlier, water is the most important part of everybody's life in this world.

No one can beat water at any stage. Water can cut through anything, water can seal anything, water can cool anything, water can create anything, water can consume anything, water can engulf anything and water can douse anything. Water can consume us is a moment and can give us life in a moment too, which is why in this country, every person prays to God with the help of water.

But the whole point of whatever I have told you is that, if we want, we can live our life without disturbing the surroundings and the surrounding environment. We are the harbingers of destruction or construction on this planet and in this life".

With this said, Guruji told Harrod that he had to meet a few other people and so Guruji left him in the garden to carry on with his activities.

Harrod went to his hut and after his dinner at 7 p.m. did some meditation and yoga exercises so that the food could get digested properly and to get a good night's sleep. All this was helping his mind become trained, focused and concentrated. Soon after, he went off to sleep.

FREEDOM IS AN APOSTLE

8

The next morning, Harrod went to the temple early and as he reached the temple, there was something that caught his eyes. It was the fishbowl. As usual, inside the bowl, there were the fishes, the plants and the water. However, he saw the whole thing from a slightly different angle. He saw all the three enshrined within the walls of the glass bowl. He knew all the three could not get out of the fishbowl how much soever they tried, till the bowl broke or someone emptied it.

Harrod became a bit disturbed. He thought about why the fishes, the plants or the water could not get out of the fishbowl and got some answers from within himself, but they were quite general. He knew if the water came out it would splash everywhere. The fishes would die if they came out of the bowl. The plants would also die if taken out of the water. But that was all he could reason.

He had to narrate all these to Guruji to get his divine intervention so he could keep his disturbing thoughts at bay.

That day he had some time to move around the ashram. He saw the ashram had a gate which was just a simple entrance, but with no doors. It was a little over a week since he had come to the ashram, and there was an urge from within to move and see the world outside the boundaries of the ashram. He wanted to step out to get a view of the world outside the ashram. As he took a step to go out, one of Guruji's disciple stopped him. During Guruji's teachings, it was his instruction not to allow anyone outside the ashram without his consent. Life inside and outside the ashram had to be kept separate for proper focus on the ashram's learning process.

Although Harrod did not get into a dispute with the disciple, he wondered why he could not go outside. He was a free bird in a free world. Why then were these bindings inside the ashram? He thought of asking Guruji that evening.

In the evening, Guruji came and took Harrod with him once again to open space. The open space was a garden filled with greenery. There were trees, flowers, green grass and an open blue sky above.

Before Harrod could say anything, Guruji asked, "Harrod, do you understand why I have brought you here."

Harrod replied, "No Guruji, I do not. I was going to ask you certain questions and suddenly you got me here."

Guruji said, "Look at the trees, the grass, they are all connected with the earth. If I were to pluck out anyone of them, it would die. But then there are ants and other insects which also live on it. If I were to take them out, they may not die. They may or may not adapt to other similar surroundings. Again, if I were to replant the grass and trees taken out, in similar surroundings they might also live, but if I pluck it out and if take time to put them back into another similar surrounding, they will surely die.

But the birds are free, they can move around to different places as they can fly. However, they also have an affinity with certain surroundings and if not suited, they might also die.

Similar to this is our fishbowl. The fishes in the water cannot live if taken out. Also, the water plants will not survive if we take them out of water. But when they both are transferred to some other similar surrounding, both of them will survive.

The fishes and the plants do not have freedom outside their natural environment. Neither do the trees, grass and flowers. Each one has to have a suitable natural surrounding for itself.

For the fishes and the plants, the current natural surrounding is the fishbowl and beyond it, they both could perish. For now, the freedom for both lies in the precinct of the water inside the bowl.

Similar to this lay our freedom limits. We are also entrapped within our social circuits, our thought process, our natural surroundings, and our very own earth. For us, every step is a step closer to our freedom.

Although we are free within our existing surroundings, we feel better when we move outside. We feel we were bound in the last place we were in. But without movement, there can be no freedom. When we free our thoughts, we invent or innovate something new. When we go beyond our homes, we discover newer places, new people, novel ways of living.

But when we keep ourselves confined within our boundaries; we can be free within it as well. There is a movement within the confined boundaries as well. Therefore, freedom is just a term that keeps us thinking beyond.

If you take a second look at the bowl, you will think about how the fishes and the plants cannot move out of it. For them, that is their world. Similarly, for us, our freedom is when we will move out of our surroundings.

But we must seek freedom with the utmost care and precaution. If we cannot explain the nature of our freedom, we will die. If the fishes jump out to attain freedom, they will die, unless there is another water body near it. Just as the fishes, we too will die if we do not take care of the perils of moving into another space.

Similar to this, is our thoughts? We only keep thinking about what we have seen, but when we free our minds, we think beyond and only then we can think more openly and deeply. We have to free our minds when we get enslaved by it. Whenever we get tired, we have to free our body of tensions, stress and exhaustion. We free our surroundings when we move out of it. We free our world when we move out of it and in all these, we must come back to the first place, that is our thoughts if we have to feel comfortable. Everything that we do outside our thought process is ultimately tied to the poles of our thought. Therefore, our freedom is actually to get out of our thoughts only.

By confining us to the world, we have learnt to look beyond it. The fishes can't think and act beyond, but we can. Things that are not free are normally non-living things. These have no necessity of moving out."

Harrod did not know, how with such ease Guruji had explained the answer to the question he had in mind. How did Guruji know about what he was thinking? How Guruji could find out exactly what he wanted? It was beyond his imagination.

So, he asked, "Guruji, this is exactly what I had in mind this morning. This is what I had seen this morning. How is it you got to know about it? I am perplexed."

Guruji smiled faintly and replied, "Harrod, this is what you call telepathy in your world. You see how well we are connected without wires. Our circuits can connect to anyone. It is for us to learn how and once we do; we will know how to know about everything that goes on in this world. But do not get to conclusions. You will know about all these as you clear your cyclic paths.

There is one more thing here. Today, you could not move out of the ashram, as the ashram is your world now. If you move out before you complete your first cycle, your thoughts will move astray and you will lose the significance of being here. Let no other thoughts occupy your mind while you are here. Once the first cycle is over, you will be free to move into your second cycle for which you will not have to stay here and will have to move out. Wait till then."

With this Guruji went away, leaving Harrod alone to ponder on whatever Guruji had said that evening.

That night, Harrod wrote in his diary:

Not Impossible

Freedom is an apostle;

Simple as it is,

Full of wisdom

And highly enjoyable.

It is like the horizon

Which is intangible,

Where the golden light

Glows and fades;

Where all directions

Seem to meet;

Which is festooned

With the powerful colours

Of the beautiful rainbow.

The further is the step,

The nearer

The terminus comes.

And!

It is a limit

The eyes can perceive.

With this written firmly in his notebook, Harrod's eyes closed and he went into a deep slumber.

THE WIRELESS CONNECTION

9

Having slept late but still having got up on time the next morning, Harrod felt a bit tired. He knew if he had to learn, it was only by following Guruji's advice. He did not know how all this would end, but something inside told him to keep going. So, after finishing his morning chores, Harrod draped the white cloth given to him by the ashram and went to the temple.

This time, between the fishes, Harrod noticed 4 green plants, and the fishes played between them as though playing hide and seek. He noticed how the fishes came near the plants and licked them, ate away the algae on them and then continued their course. While the plants swayed along with the fishes, Harrod wondered what was it that gave life to these plants inside water. There was no soil and no air, just water. Still, the plants lived on in the depths of the water with no other life support systems. What made them live with the fishes and were these plants destined to live with the fishes as well. Were the fishes providing life support to the plants also!

Harrod was just 30 years of age, a young boy just out of his college and with little hands-on experience. He was still checking out his career options after his small stint at different science laboratories when he got the call from Guruji. But somewhere his sub-conscious mind spoke and told him that this was an important aspect of his life and he must, therefore, stay there. He was young & ambitious but some supernatural power was pulling him back to continue to stay at the ashram. He did not know what or who, but anyway, stayed.

With Guruji's daily guidance, he was now getting deeper into the depths of his mind, only by just observing the bowl. How could these co-exist, how was life breathing into them- the only common medium being water between them? Well, just as Guruji had explained, and he had also read in his classes, water made up two-thirds of the earth and almost everything on this earth comprised similar proportions. He was getting to the root. Water was essential for the survival of the fishes and the plants.

That morning, Harrod was thrilled, he had discovered the essence of some of his observations. He was eager to tell Guruji. He thought Guruji would be thrilled about this, and he was yearning to hear it from him.

As soon as he met Guruji that evening, he told him about all his observations and what he thought would be the meaning of it. Guruji listened to Harrod calmly as he spoke. Once Harrod had spoken, Guruji smiled and said, "Harrod, you have observed well today, but you must understand the fact, that, though things are so simple in life, the derivations are not. Think deeper to understand it all".

"Harrod", Guruji continued, "What you have seen is a mere connection between the plants, water and the fishes. The fishes are wirelessly connected to the plants, and the medium is water. They have been made to survive in this manner. We do not know what they speak, but if you keep on observing minutely, you might decipher it one day. The fishes can live without the plants and so can the plants live without them, but both will die if they leave the medium, which is water. But the fishes eat from the plants and when they swim vigorously through the water, it makes the plant sway along with the water and in the process cleans the plants too. The fishes help the plants clean up by eating the algae, and the algae on the plants is a source of food for the fishes as well. They are both interconnected.

Both of them live with the help of water and air. Without these two factors, we too shall not be able to live even a single second. People will tell you we can exist only when we have a combination of earth and fire with water and air. But if you were to see astronauts, they survive only with the help of these two ingredients when in space. Do they need earth and fire there? If they have a strong will, they could survive for days together with these two vital ingredients i.e., water and air. Without these two, none of the living things could survive even a single moment. But in space, the astronauts are connected to them as their space stations are made of matter from the earth and fire keeps the engine running within their body and also the space engines. So, each one is so intricately connected to the other.

But the connection is important. The fishes are also connected with the plants and earth and whatever there is near them in their natural environment. So, we need these in our natural environment. The fishes breathe the air from the water with the help of gills, and the plants do so in their way. So, the air is prevalent everywhere in some form or the other.

What we need to learn here is that the environment is a vital factor in our lives. We are connected by it wirelessly. We do not know how, but this is a powerful medium. Air is a medium. God has provided the medium with its natural flavours for us to relish. We cannot and should not pollute it. When I say we cannot, I mean that even if we pollute, there are natural mechanisms that will first help prevent it and if it can't then the factors of adjustability come into force. The earth will buckle and bend under pressure, there will be storms, tsunamis, typhoons, earthquakes, volcanic eruptions which will destroy everything, but in the process will give new life to the earth in the future. We will all die, but the earth will survive after cleaning its environment. It has done so for billions of years and will continue to do so. We need to protect our present to secure the future of our generations.

God has devised ways for all of us to live, but it is for us to choose how. We need to understand the mystery of God himself when he dreamt of creating the universe and did it with such perfection. We have no right to destroy what God has made. God will ultimately prevail, but we shall be the losers ourselves.

The same is true not just in the world of nature, but within our worlds as well. We are all connected through the medium of our nature. We must protect everything and since we are the only species with the most developed brains, it is our responsibility to see that everything is protected".

Harrod had learnt the lesson for the day and that night, Harrod after penning down Guruji's sermon, wrote in his diary:

<u>Playgrounds of Time</u>

The prevailing air

Maladjusted by atomicity,

Has carried,

Excruciating tortures;

Made the juvenile

Responsible,

For every act of time;

Created blaspheming fate

For the paupers;

Challenged the populace,

To defy nature;

Pressed the world

Into a massive hole,

To make it a slave

Of the chariots of time.

And!

It is at that point

Of prolific stagnation

Where I stand

And,

Deliver my speech.

Harrod could not sleep that night. He sat outside his cottage, looking at the vast expanse of the sky. He thought of God and how God had created such a huge empire, where everything was so meticulously controlled. How had he made man desperate to think about his works of art? How had God provided a small part of himself in creating smaller versions of himself at every place?

On the other hand, he also thought about the marvels being created by man himself. The man had created many things. First, they were rugged, then mechanical, then they became electrical and then there was an improvement in electronics with circuits and now everything was getting connected wirelessly. He thought about gadgets such as computers, mobile phones, microphones, television, satellites, rockets and likewise various other radio-controlled instruments being used wirelessly. Humans were moving towards materialistic wireless possibilities which could be destroyed anytime and here was Guruji explaining the human way of wireless connection which would get better and better with more use. It was beyond anything that humankind could create.

Harrod had been a part of the present world in its entirety, and he knew what man could do. But Guruji was taking him towards a step closer to his inner world's wireless possibilities. If we can achieve this, there would be limitless boundaries for us.

DREAMS ARE POWERFUL THOUGHT

REPLAYS

10

Harrod felt drowsy when he woke up the following morning. He had not slept throughout the night but dozed off at the onset of dawn. He overslept till eight in the morning and when he got up; it surprised him to hear the voice of Guruji's disciples chanting mantras. Guruji's small group of disciples had all gone through the program which Harrod was going through now. They had learnt the first cycle of life. He knew he was late, but without wasting a minute he finished his morning chores. He then went to the place where the other disciples had gathered. As per the rules of the ashram, the disciples could only perform the duties as per the instructions which Guruji had left for them. Unknowingly Harrod wandered to the temple when one disciple stopped him. As he was already late he was asked to go back, citing Guruji's instruction. Even though Harrod felt annoyed at the harsh treatment, he could do nothing about it and therefore went back to his cottage, not wanting his actions to hurt Guruji.

Harrod came back to his cottage, sat down in the lotus posture, and chanted the AUM mantra alone for around an hour. After this, he meditated for another half an hour and then had some fruits and milk for breakfast. From time to time, the breakfast menu would change, but it would be simple and healthy. Harrod yearned to have his favourite food - coffee, bread toast, puddings, non-vegetarian food; but knew very well that he had to live the simple life of the ashram if he had to stay there and learn. It was taking him time to understand everything, but he wanted to learn fast, just like most of them there, had already done. He wanted the shortcut method, but then Guruji's words sounded from within himself– "There are no shortcuts in life, live every moment that has been allocated to you. Your life's software has been written and no one can change it. You can improve upon the features, but the basics have been determined. Every breadth has been measured, although you can still control the breadth for your benefit. You are here, not because you wanted to come here, but because you were destined".

Guruji would always talk in the simplest of words, and Harrod would often wonder how Guruji could take everything in such a light note. Life had lots of difficulties, but Guruji seemed to have every answer to it. He could explain almost everything so simply, yet so realistically. Guruji was educated and had read all the religious and other thought-provoking and educational books by the greatest authors of the world. He could always express everything with such ease that anybody could understand it in the minutest amount of time. He was simple, his ashram was simple depicting his reflection and taste, and he also asked his disciples to replicate the same.

After each disciple had gone through the course or the principles laid out by Guruji, they could go anywhere they liked, but as Guruji wanted, they were bound by the promise to preach whatever they had learnt in the ashram, to the people across the world. He never asked his disciples to drop the profession they were pursuing as Guruji considered that too, a part of their destiny. But after being at the ashram and undergoing Guruji's teachings, there were hardly any who had gone back to their previous life of worldly pleasure. The simplicity of the ashram was enough to bring them to their knees, make them like it, and help them become a part of it.

Guruji's ashram ran like many other ashrams, with the help of donations from people who were staunch followers of Guruji. The devotees would come to the ashram once a year and donate whatever they could for the well-being of the ashram. Guruji would bless them all. Similarly, Guruji had created a system for his disciples by which they could get alms from people everywhere. Since the 4 cycles being taught were arduous, there were only a few disciples who could get through all of them, but those who did clear the first cycle went to different places to preach whatever they had learnt at the ashram.

So, after Harrod had his breakfast, he went back to his cottage and thought about what he would tell Guruji in the evening. He had missed one day's observation of the fishes. He thought and thought, but just could not come to any definite conclusion that would spur him to put up questions about the fishes and the bowl to Guruji. Thinking about all this, he suddenly dozed off and dreamt about the fishes, the bowl, the water, the plants, the temple and Guruji sitting right in front of him. He could see everything crystal clear as if he was there himself. Guruji was smiling, and the divine smile was sweeter than anything Harrod had ever experienced. The fishes were swimming, and they were also smiling. The plants were swaying, and it looked as though there was a smile on them too. So was the case with water and the bowl also, and they too looked as though they were smiling. Everything around him looked fresher than ever. There was as if an aura of God himself.

After being asleep for almost an hour, he suddenly woke up and found himself once again in his cottage, instead of the temple he had seen in his dreams. He wondered and started recalling every moment of his dream. But as he did so, he could not understand the significance of all this. He got up, washed his face and then went to the cottage where lunch was being served.

All the disciples were already sitting in four rows and there were volunteers from among the disciples who were serving the food. Harrod took his seat, and he was served yellow lentil, rice, a thin watery semi-liquid made with dates and some vegetable curries. He ate his lunch and at the end, he also got some sweet rice as dessert.

After lunch, however, all disciples would go back to their respective cottages and rest for one hour and then get back to their routine jobs. Every evening at seven, Guruji would give a sermon for an hour and then the disciples would disperse for their dinner and evening prayers. But then, each disciple also had their daily routine outlined, and for each one, it was laid down differently.

As usual, at 5 p.m., he met Guruji in the garden. Guruji had developed a habit to be with his favourite disciples during this time. Just like Harrod, many disciples had come and gone, and Harrod considered himself very fortunate to be one who was blessed by Guruji himself amongst so many.

Like always, on meeting Guruji, Harrod paid his respects to him and Guruji asked, "So Harrod, what did you observe today".

Harrod said, "Guruji, I am sorry I got up late in the morning as I slept late yesterday. I engrossed the entire evening with your teachings in my mind. Therefore, today I could observe nothing".

But then Guruji asked, "Okay, not the fishes, but Harrod, have you not observed anything else during the day"?

Was Guruji hinting at something? Harrod thought.

He thought over and then said, "No Guruji, nothing else except for the daily routine activities that we go through".

Guruji said, "Think again" and walked ahead.

Harrod's mind raced, but he could recall nothing. Suddenly his mind flashed, and he got so excited by it he nearly fell off. He ran to Guruji and said, "Guruji, I recall having a dream today" and he explained every aspect of the dream. He then continued, "But Guruji, I could not find any reason for this dream, so I did not tell it to you. When you insisted, I had a feeling that this is what you wanted to hear. If I am correct, tell me Guruji, what was so special about my dream".

Finally, Guruji explained, "Harrod, you are correct. Dreams are the manifestations of the daily activities of people. They are vibrations happening inside everyone. We relate them to activities that you have sometimes thought about unknowingly and which linger on at the back of your mind. Sometimes, however, you can also control your dreams. Like today, even though unconsciously, you had the repentance of not going to the temple in the morning. The thought got ingrained in your brain and this thought was focused and repeated in your dream. You wanted to see the temple, the fishes, the plants, the water, the bowl and you could see it in your dreams. It is not always that the dreams come to you on the same day when the events have occurred, but these kinds of thoughts remain in your subconscious mind and come back in your dreams in the weirdest of times and forms. But today, your thought process wanted you to meet me with something, as you had nothing to narrate. There was a sense of fear which triggered the dream. But there was a difference. You saw everything smiling in your dream. It was to cut your miseries which you were going through today and to make you understand that the entire world could smile if you wanted it to. It is your action that makes the world smile or makes it sad, and one could only smile if one learnt how to smile himself. Be not afraid of anything if you are on the right path. Smile your way through life and you find that everything on this earth and outside will have no choice but to smile back and guide you along.

Today you missed your morning class (class because it is something, I have made mandatory for you to learn), despite that, you would learn something important, as you desired it to happen. Unknowingly things happened just because your thought process was so strong that it overcame all other factors that could obstruct it. You had to learn the lesson of smiling today and you did.

Tomorrow when you go to the temple, smile at the fishes and the bowl and the water and the plants and whosoever comes in your path and see how you are rewarded.

Harrod, a smile is something that can change the way you look at life. When you saw the fishes today, they seemed to smile; the plants seemed to smile; the bowl seemed to smile, and the water seemed to smile. Everything that you saw, smiled, and the smile attracted you so much that you wanted to remember what you saw in your dreams. It is not always that one remembers one's dreams, but you did it so vividly that you could bring forth the entire picture in front of me. It left an impact on you. Inertly, you also wanted to smile as they did.

You must remember to always smile internally and not just externally. The smile that comes from within you resonates automatically on your face and your body. The inner smile will strike anyone at the heart and everyone will feel comfortable being with you. However, an outer smile, which is superficial, is easily recognizable, will be temporary and only attract someone for a short period.

Smile is something that we must all learn to do. If we observe properly, we can also see the ferocious lions and tigers smile, even though they are a terror for us. Your heart must smile, your mind must smile, and your body must also smile. You see it will get automatically reflected on your face, your eyes, your lips and your skin will glow. People will love to sit next to you just because you would sound and look so fresh to them. You could win over anyone with just one smile. Some people kill by using weapons, but you can kill with their smile too."

Guruji smiled at Harrod, and he could understand what Guruji had just narrated. He left Harrod for the day.

Harrod also smiled, and he knew instantly that this was something that came from within him, and he must do everything to keep this inner warmth and smile actively with him.

How could Guruji come to know about his dream, and how had he interpreted it so nicely? It was as though Guruji knew he had missed his morning ritual and so had come to him in his dreams to teach him the day's lesson.

While Harrod thought about what wonderful things he had learnt that day, it was time for his dinner and he could feel the pangs in his stomach.

Harrod continued to the dining room where once again other disciples had gathered just like him. They all sat in four long rows and were served their food. Dinner was simple with rice and a vegetable mixture, which everyone called khichdi. It was very refreshing, and the stomach felt full after just one serving. Harrod had some water. Dinner lasted for twenty minutes and then Harrod left for his cottage.

That night Harrod slept peacefully. There was something that he had accomplished. He smiled while he lay asleep and anyone who would have seen him that night, would have certainly felt the power of his smile in the coolness of his sleep.

EVERY ACTION HAS A REACTION

11

The next morning, Harrod once again sat near the fishbowl and watched the fishes swimming happily. As the days went by, he saw the water inside the bowl getting murkier. Like the earth's ocean floor, there were deposits at the bottom of the fishbowl too. The water had not been cleaned for some time, unlike the earth which keeps churning to stay fresh. There was no filter system to get the water automatically cleaned from the system. How would the fish survive if the water got toxic by their faeces? There was no other way by which they could make the water fresh for the fishes apart from cleaning it. If this continued, the polluted water could kill the fishes after some more time there. Harrod could do nothing about it, but ask Guruji regarding cleaning of the fishbowl, as without Guruji's instructions nothing could move inside the ashram. He did not like the dirty water and this incidence tore the smile away from his face.

The whole day, this thought kept Harrod worried till finally, he met Guruji. As soon as he met him, Harrod

asked Guruji to get the water cleaned inside the bowl.
Guruji asked, "Why, what happened, Harrod?"

Harrod explained that his morning observation was about
the fishes' life and that they would die in the dirty water.
Therefore, they should change the water. Even the plants
could die soon if they failed to take care of it.

Guruji remained calm and heard Harrod patiently. He then
said, "Harrod, it was good you noticed this, as today, after
you left the temple, I got the water changed. Right now,
the fishes and the plants are in freshwater. If you had not
observed today, you would have missed this opportunity."

It was as though everything was exactly framed for
Harrod. He was destined to notice this event that day.

Harrod asked Guruji what was so special about the
morning's observation, that he could have missed if he
had not observed it on that day.

Guruji explained, "If today you had not observed then,
tomorrow this opportunity could not have come back for
you. You are here in the first cycle for a set number of
days, which you will understand as time goes by. As a
regularly scheduled system, we get the water cleaned, the
bowl & plants washed so that everything inside it becomes
fresh and this time it was your turn to see and understand
its significance. So, your observation of today's event was
perfect and on time.

This has relevance to our daily lives as well. It is
connected to us directly. Nature has provided us with
seasons, weathers, climatic changes and each has its
systems inter-woven so finely and infinitely with the other

systems that they perform their scheduled tasks regularly and each system self-cleans itself.

We, as part of the living things on earth, are also creators of the dirt and filth everywhere. Of course, animals would only do so through the means that they have learnt, but their act is limited. But a man with his mind and immense capabilities is capable of a much larger danger to mother earth. Man uploads the dirt in different forms, and nature shakes and cleans it every time. In the process, however, lots of lives are lost. Whereas at one place, we care for the bowl and the fishes as there is no self-cleansing system; we fail to care for the earth as it cares for itself whenever there is any danger posed to its inbuilt systems. We may die, but nature will survive for the future of life on this planet and the survival of the solar system.

Just like our bodies have got internal systems as organs, nerves, blood vessels-which keep on working daily even though we may go to sleep or work, similarly nature also has its ecosystems working day and night to care for everything it has on its lap."

Harrod understood the significance of the observation. From his childhood, he knew he had to go to the toilet every day, but little did he wonder about the importance of the entire system. He started understanding the earth's intrinsic system that every inlet has to have an outlet. Just as the fishes got their discharge after eating, so did the plants let go carbon-dioxide while taking in oxygen and vice versa, and so did the earth for its various resources to get itself replenished.

Guruji continued, "Harrod, everything that we do, has an exact repercussion on this earth's ecological system. We as individuals do small things which are lost in the earth's vastness. But when we collectively challenge nature, then nature has no other option but to accept the challenge. When it does so, it does with all its might. In the process, we and all other living things bear nature's vengeance and its brunt leaves us torn and shattered."

"Come here and I will show you how we are destroying the earth by polluting it," Guruji said. He continued, "We are bringing destruction to our own lives. In the process of comforting our present and satisfying our hidden desires, we are destroying our very own future."

He held Harrod's hand and took him to the pond next to the garden.

Guruji said, "Harrod see this very simple thing. This is a pond, just a bigger version of the fishbowl. This is surrounded by grass and trees. Birds come here to quench their thirst and smaller animals come here also to enjoy themselves and quench their thirst or hunger. It is home to everybody. We too come here to breathe fresh air and refresh our lungs. The fishes inside the pond live a larger life inside. We all enjoy this place. This place has meaning for us. But this place is also a protected place, as it is within the precincts of the ashram boundary wall.

But as we see this, we also see people who would like to fish here for filling their stomach's urge and others come here to make a living by cutting the grass, catching and selling the fishes. There are still others who come here with other thoughts in mind, like taking a morning walk around the pond for refreshing their lungs and yet others who would like to clean themselves, or practice swimming. So, there are various uses of just one of the very many natural creations of Mother Nature. Of course, man could also make this pond, but mostly it would be a natural one.

Again, others would come to the pond to understand how much money they could earn by filling up the pond and making a concrete structure over it. By doing this they would earn money, but in the process would destroy a unique feature of nature by building a concrete jungle. By doing this they would make money and become wealthy, but in the process, they would also take away the freshness that this place once used to provide to so many people and living beings. Each one of these livings beings that frequent this spot would disappear from this place, as they would then look at other options for performing the same daily activities that they once practised here.

Harrod, can you imagine just a small place like this could wreak havoc for the environment if the rules being made by man meddled it? We are all here because Mother Nature wants us to. If Mother Nature would decide, we could all die within seconds? Man is trying to become the Father of Mother Nature and is creating its biggest mistake in doing so. We must all look up to go forward, but we must never stop looking down also, as it is on nature, that we build our fortunes. Our roots have to be secure first."

Guruji continued, "Harrod, man is subject to the forces of nature. Not that nature will overlook man's requirement, but if man would continue to destroy nature's wealth, nature will have no choice but to rectify the process, and during this process, living things would get destroyed. It is not by chance that the great Vedas & Upanishads have been written, but the great gurus of the yesteryears had experienced this, by either way of reality or through foresight. They have written about the various ages that the earth will undergo, and this is now becoming a reality. Man is making it a reality through his actions.

Harrod, we have to do everything to protect our environment. It is the need of the day. With man constructing things to protect himself, he is also creating the same things to destroy himself. I know it is difficult for a single person to convince the world about this, but we have to make a joint effort. We must use everything in our power to make the world aware of the anomalies that the earth is facing. I will come to other factors later, but you must promise today to educate the world in masses and not just educate, but attempt to ingrain the basis of all these into their brains. If you observe well, everywhere you go, you will find examples of the destruction of nature's wealth, which has been provided abundantly to us by Mother Earth, and we must all do whatever we can to help it upkeep its balance.

Just imagine, if you were to listen to me only and then go away, forgetting everything, what use would the knowledge be that I am imparting. But if you would learn and use it sincerely, then don't you think that the world would be a better place to live in."

Harrod nodded. He was listening intently and trying to understand the significance of nature more closely.

Guruji said, "I have been telling you about various things that the fishes have been teaching you and this will continue for some more time. I understand you are getting involved and learning every day. I know you are deep in your thoughts after talking to me every day, but think, if you would not, then can you learn and teach others as well? Once you complete your time here, I urge you to take it upon yourself to educate people around the world to learn the important things in life and practice them in person. Humans forget whatever they learn, but you must try to change the subconscious mind of the people by your words and only then would they be able to recognize the importance of what I am explaining to you today.

Harrod, if you have noticed a small child, he will learn things if he likes, but once he does, he will remember it throughout his life. The thoughts have been engrained in his sub-conscious mind during the fresh first few years of his life. So even though his later actions would be because of his interactions with his peers and friends, his subconscious mind will always remind him of the wrong and about the values that he has learnt during his childhood and prevent him from digressing."

Guruji left for the day with these words.

Harrod had known about the sub-conscious mind, but he got engrossed in his thoughts about how to make it work. He had also attended various lectures on this by religious and academic teachers. Harrod had learnt to reason, but how could he affect and enter the minds of other people. He was not a magician, but he knew whatever Guruji was asking him to do was very much within his purview and what he was destined to do. Probably whatever Guruji was teaching him here would enable him to carry forward the work that Guruji had lined up for him!

In the meantime, Harrod was also learning the power of concentration, meditation and other forms of reasoning methods at Guruji's ashram. His daily activities and exercises were providing him with new insights into the new world, which Guruji was inclined to teach him about.

In Guruji's teachings, Harrod was learning to understand the importance of destiny as well. There was something that was constantly changing Harrod's mind. There were various simultaneous permutations and combinations taking place in his small but vast brain. In a few days, the change being made in his mind, was just like the earth refreshing itself for correcting the anomalies in its systems.

RELEVANCE OF THE FISHES

12

During his daily visits to the temple, Harrod enjoyed playing with the fishes. His liking grew more and more, every time both came near each other. Each day he started seeing something new which the fishes were trying to teach him. Since every morning Harrod had the duty to observe the fishes, give them some food pills and then wait and watch what new gifts they had for him, he thought of becoming friends with them and learning their ways in the water.

The following morning, without Guruji's knowledge, Harrod lifted the fishbowl from its stand and took it outside the temple, kept it in the morning sunlight. But one of the temple disciples saw it and told Harrod that the fishes dislike the sun and they are not supposed to be brought out of the temple without Guruji's instruction. But Harrod wanted to understand what made them stay away from the sunlight. While he kept the bowl in the bright morning sunlight, he saw the fishes, first wriggle and then dance, but after some time he saw them hide in the shade of the plants inside. The sunlight was too warm, and they could not tolerate the brilliance of the sunlight. It was like him standing outside in the sun during summer and after sometime wanting some shade because of the extreme heat. While living in the water was quite peculiar, Harrod thought of the ways God had created every life in its selected surroundings. While the sun sprayed its light, helping the water and the fishes shine, it also made the fishes shy of the sunlight. Feeling bad, after a few minutes he brought the bowl inside the temple and placed it back on the wooden stand where he could see them jump and bounce and feel the joy of the shade once again. He could see even with no kind of formal education; the fishes were still enjoying the power and joy of being together and also understanding the meaning of light and shade. This play was usual for them. He made another observation during this time that these fishes would never fight over anything. Of course, looking at the size of the bowl, he could understand why there weren't any larger fishes in the bowl that could instigate a fight.

As though a new light had been shown on him, Harrod thought about reasons the fishes in the bowl would not fight with each other in the bowl. He concluded:

a) There was not much difference in their sizes.

b) They all wanted the same food.

c) They were all thrilled in this kind of environment.

d) There was just the requisite number of fishes in the bowl. No overcrowding.

What if there were larger fishes than the ones currently there or some more fish in the bowl? - There would be utter chaos. The larger fishes would either gobble the smaller ones or eat the food which was meant for the smaller ones. If the smaller fishes were not able to eat, then they would eventually die. This gave insights to Harrod on why God made the larger ponds, rivers, seas and oceans. They were meant for creatures that could not fit into the bowl and which gave them food according to their size and habitat. But this was not the end. He was sensing other things could enable him to understand nature, but at the moment all his questions and answers lay with the fishes in the bowl.

Harrod could understand that just like the ponds, rivers, lakes and oceans were created for the larger aquatic creatures, so it was true, vice versa as well. Could it be that the fishes were created only to fully complete the ponds, rivers, lakes and help the water stay alive? Whereas the smaller fishes could adapt to any water body, the larger fishes could only adapt to where they could fit in.

That day Harrod was happy that the fishbowl had helped him identify some of nature's secrets. Although all this seemed quite simple for him, he could also understand that within what he had seen and understood that day, there was something amiss, something much deeper which he had to learn from this episode. So, he waited for Guruji to tell him about his observation and what he had learnt.

As usual, Guruji came to the garden at 5 p.m. and saw Harrod waiting impatiently. Guruji asked, "Harrod, what is in your mind and what is it you want to ask? You seem to be very impatient today?"

Harrod narrated the whole incident and what he had deciphered from the episode. Guruji patiently heard him and he could sense that every word was being consumed by Guruji as he was narrating it.

Finally, when the narration was complete, Guruji spoke, "Harrod, you have observed few things well today and so too was your inference from what you observed. However, you have not related this to nature and the humans on this planet, or the universe. You have only looked at the fishes and how it survives in the bowl or the larger water bodies."

"No Guruji! I had the feeling that fishes are a part of nature and whatever I saw was nature itself. So, what else could I learn from nature? As far as humans are concerned, there is some connection, as they are both a part of this world and also constantly improvising themselves for moving into the vast space of the universe. So, nature has a different meaning for them. But how could the fishes teach me more about the universe?" Harrod asked inquisitively.

Guruji cleared, "Harrod, think about what would happen if these fishes were not in the lap of Mother Nature. With the fishes, God has created:

1. Food for the Fishes themselves.

2. Food for animals and humans.

3. The colours of the fauna which makes us understand colours can exist in water as well, even though water washes away everything, with time.

4. Providing life in water.

5. Making the water livelier.

6. Making us understand that life can co-exist in water as well.

7. Making us confident in exploring the depths of the water.

8. Providing us with a positive attitude.

9. Making us understand that big and small can co-exist in the same environment.

10. Giving us insights into the wonder that is nature.

With all these, God has made us more daring; provided more colours into our life; made us fill our stomachs; made us understand that breathing is an exercise which is performed not just by the animal kingdom; has created the goal that we all need to breathe to live and survive - just as fishes in the water - but through different ways and means; has made us understand that oil is also a part of our existence- we got this knowledge when we knew how to extract oil from some fishes as well.

So, fishes have given us a lot. Although what I will provide you, will be the tip of the iceberg, you will understand more, when you read more and more of the ancient sciences and learn to understand the nature of the earth and its survival methods. Let me delve into some more depth on this topic."

Harrod knew he had to learn a lot more from what he had observed that day, and Guruji was proving him right. The topic of the fishes had taken a new turn.

Guruji continued, "Harrod, let me take oil for an example. We now know that oil is a part of every living mechanism. We can find oil in the soil, beneath the soil, in the fishes, in the plants, in the animals and within ourselves as well. You see that our skin pores always secrete some kind of oil, and on dry skin, we have to apply some oil to keep it looking fresh. Oil is a very important ingredient for the earth and Mother Nature has seen that, that just as water, air and sunlight, there is no dearth of it. But water, air, sunlight are renewable resources. Although oil also is renewable, the pace is rather slow. Water has its cycle of renewal daily, the air has its cycle within the limits of the earth's atmosphere, and the sunlight is permanent till one day we do something to destroy its vigour.

Oil as we all know is being used by us in different forms. We are using oil for our body, for running machines, for running vehicles and for various other applications which keep the world's economy running. Due to reasons of its various applications today, we can't imagine the world without oil.

Have you noticed that if you had no oil in your food for some days, what would happen to your body? Your body would start losing its lustre and there will come a time when your body skin will dry up and you would end up having a lot of different ailments. Just as the earth, our body also can build its resources of oil, but no one knows how to manage the same in our body systems. It is also an art to know how to manage our body oil parameters. But only a few who have studied and practised well would know how to keep the body healthy without food and oil.

When we are discussing here, we are talking about the common people, who are not aware that their actions can cause Mother Nature to shrivel and I want them to understand that oil is an important ingredient for Mother Nature just as it is for us. Note Harrod, that the entire world is extracting oil from any place that it is getting– earth, sea, plants, animals, fishes. The extraction has been increasing every day and nature has till now supported man's cause. But till when! We must understand that it takes millions of years for the earth to generate the resources it has, and we would destroy it within a few decades. We must also understand that the earth is composed of matter, which keeps it performing its duty of rotation and revolution. It is with the help of this matter that earth keeps itself constant in this orbit and balances with other planets. Let not the forces of nature play havoc with humanity because of the small inhibitions of this present race.

Harrod, can you imagine your body without oil or the minerals that compose your body? Would you live without them? Similarly, if we were to extract all the oil and minerals from this world and destroy its nature, could earth survive? We must learn to use the richer renewable resources to power our systems, and oil is surely not one of them. We must understand that when we use nature's non-renewable resources, we are transferring these from one place to another in different forms on this planet. In time, this will cause an imbalance in the resources of one place with the other. Nature will not sit back and watch. The consequences of this are already there to see and it will be disastrous. The ocean currents are changing, the tectonic plates beneath the earth's surface are moving and buckling, the weather worldwide is changing, the earth is getting warmer and there will be one day when it will super cool itself after a show of super warming. Where will all these lead to?

We keep on hearing the end of the world is coming, and so it will if we were to exploit Mother Nature's resources scrupulously. The earth will keep on balancing whenever there is a gap created on it and will therefore destroy anything that comes in touch with it. We must understand, to just make our present successful, we shouldn't destroy the future of this planet. Once the planet wobbles to adjust to the gaps created by us, it is almost certain that the entire nature on this planet will get destroyed and the end is not very far away, if we continue on this path. I can see that the day is not far when we will see the consequences of our actions.

As I have told you before, our body is a smaller manifestation of the earth and the earth is a smaller manifestation of the galaxy and so is the galaxy of the universe. Each of the smaller ones must derive its strength from resources provided by the greater one, and thus we derive our resources from what earth has, and the earth derives it from the galaxy it is in and so does the galaxy from the universe. Similarly, each larger object is a derivation of the smaller ones. Thus, each one is infinitely connected with the other by its natural resources. If it disturbs anyone, it will be like the same poles of two different magnets, when in contact with each other. They will bounce and dislodge instead of sticking together."

"Harrod," Guruji continued, "I hope you have understood the importance of oil on this earth and our body, but we have more lessons to be learnt from today's observation. The devastation will happen because of our activities, but for a brighter future, we must try to protect anything and everything important on this earth."

It was a long evening and Guruji asked Harrod to come back the next day for further insights into the day's observation.

THE BALANCE OF NATURE

13

The following evening, Harrod approached Guruji again. As Harrod entered the room, he saw Guruji sitting cross-legged with his eyes closed, deep in his meditation. Harrod did not want to disturb Guruji and so he sat at the entrance waiting for Guruji to complete his meditation and open his eyes.

For the next half-hour, Guruji sat there and Harrod watched him with great concentrations. He saw Guruji's resplendent face, his calm composure and the great calmness and the light which came from within. He could recognize it instantly. There was some kind of illumination which came from within Guruji as if there was something more to him than he could perceive.

Finally, when Guruji opened his eyes, he saw Harrod sitting in front of him. Guruji smiled and called Harrod next to him. Harrod walked inside slowly, and Guruji recalled whatever he had told him on the previous day. Guruji spoke once again on the subject.

"Harrod, all the species on this planet are divided into good and evil, into black and white, into big and small, sweet and salty. If there were fishes in the bowl of a different nature, there would have been a war for the survival of the fittest. But you find there are fishes only of the same species, in this bowl. I have purposely kept it that way so that it reminds us of the fact that good can survive alone. If I were to keep more of the attacking fishes, then the good ones would not have survived and it would have ruined the very purpose of the bowl. But remember, bad is as good for the earth as the good itself, as it keeps reminding us that we should be good. Also, we would not have known what is bad or what the opposite of good is, if there was no bad. Bad motivates us to remain good. It provides us with a sense of acting humane in times of need. The purpose of telling you all this is, if we were not good, we would not be helping others. Within every being on this planet, is the good and the evil, and it is upon us to decide what we want to be and decide the reason for it. Each individual decides what he wants to do in life and if you closely watch, you find that whatever he does is again related to something good or evil, based on his/her circumstances.

There is a balance of everything in this huge universal system. If the good has been created, so is evil created. Similarly, is the case of black and white; big and small. For everything that is created, there are two sides to it. One portrays the positive side and the other shows the negative side. This is also part of the universal truth, and we must all perceive everything in this manner. But our minds are subject to weakness' and we get attracted to it quickly. So, we must always try to look at the positive side, even when circumstances lead us to think on a negative one. This will help us reach the brighter side fast and when we do so, we will find solutions to the problems, rather than delve into problems."

Guruji pointed to another fact.

"Harrod, you have rightly pointed out the facts of why only the requisite number of fishes should be there in the bowl. If there would be more, there would be chaos, confusion, war and the likeliness that the bowl would topple one day because of the eagerness of the larger fishes to overthrow the inferior ones and to find more space for themselves. So the explanation is true for this world, this planet earth and the universe. If we were to take the earth as an example, there is enough space for billions of people to stay here, but the earth has been divided into different zones–land and water, fertile and non-fertile or arid land, plains, deserts and the mountains, hard and soft soil, hot and the cold, the big and the small, the calm and the disturbing zones. Each of these has been separated so that our population does not multiply indefinitely and the earth can adjust itself to any circumstance to regain its posture if someone violates the basic principle of staying here, whether it be the humans, animals, plants, fishes or anything else. Nature is by default ready to put in checks at places where there is an imbalance, and when it does so, we must endure it. Just like the cells in our body, humans too can multiply indiscriminately, so can animals, plants and fishes or birds. There is freedom provided to everyone on this planet. But only humans can understand the reasons and can put in the required checks. But we all live with our selfish motive of self-fulfilment and therefore, cannot understand the true underlying principles."

Guruji continued, "We have been sent to this earth to help nature in its endeavour and to serve all the species here in your special way. Since we have been bestowed with the power of knowledge and to invent, innovate and construct anything that we want above every other species, we should not do anything, to destroy whatever Mother Earth has given us. But instead, we should devise ways in which we could preserve nature's way so that it could work towards our advantage and for all the species at large. If we were only to look at our freedom, then what can we do to protect the freedom of this earth. As we depend on the earth, so is this earth dependent upon us to survive in this solar system, and so does this solar system depend on the earth to survive in this universe. We are so closely connected with each other that we all should only act in unison so that Mother Earth could proudly narrate its proud story to its other brothers and sisters that no one can do anything to destroy its existence till we are there to care for it. Humans must analyse why they should survive and why the earth should also survive. Let us work on matters beyond our thoughts, on matters which require the broader perspective of looking beyond just us, beyond the earth, beyond the planets, beyond the solar system, beyond the galaxies, beyond the milky way's, beyond the stars and the universe. Let us bring care into the entire system of our existence.

Harrod, you must have noted the various points that I have explained to you why the existence of the fishes on this earth was so important. With the fishes, God created food for the fishes, for the animal kingdom and the kingdom of the birds. The fishes are as important for the plants as the plant is for them. So, it is true for animals and birds. It is a natural process that within the fishes there are vegetarians and non-vegetarians, so it is also true in the animal kingdom. Some survive on plants and others who survive on both plants and animals, while there are still others who survive on animals. For us, it is an instinct that has been taught by the seniors to their juniors and so the tradition continues, till someone realizes that this is no right or wrong. That one soul is eating into another is not the true nature of mother earth, but just as I said, the good and the bad need to coexist to maintain the balance. But if you now look at the brighter side, fishes who live on plants survive the same way that fishes who survive on other fishes do. So why should we keep on killing other souls to survive ourselves? It is only the wish to keep eating that drives us to kill. Can we survive, if we could control the very thought of eating? I have the answer, but I will delve on it at an appropriate date and time sometime later," Guruji told Harrod.

Guruji continuing on his earlier point and said, "Harrod, let us look at the other points of your observation. What would happen if there were no colours? The world would be black and white like the universe itself. As I told you earlier, everything on this earth is divided into black and white and so is in the universe. If we look into space at night, we find the universe has lots of stars and planets which keep shining white and the rest of the space is black. But within all these, there are places like the earth which are festooned with colours. From a distance, we cannot observe it, but when we get closer, the significance of the colours is so apparent.

Similarly, this is the case with Earth. Within earth itself, there is everything in black and white; black and white people, black and white fishes, black and white animals, black and white days and nights respectively, black and white insects, black and white water, but within every black and white is a dash of colour to bring out its brilliance. So is the significance of the fishes, along with the fauna, to provide the shine from within. Similar are the colours on mother nature to provide the shine from within, to make us understand that our life is not black and white but decorated with colours and we must recognize this. Colours provide vibrancy to our lives and without them, our world would have been just black or white. Colours prove the fact that we can change our lives to improve or destroy them. It is the selection of colours that keep us running and once the colour fades, our lives also end. Everything in our lives is from white to black and colours are there to fathom it.

So is the case of nature and earth. If we, with our selfish acts, destroy the colours ourselves on this earth, we will kill the living instinct of nature and therefore, kill earth itself. Let us improve the colours of nature, let us improve the colours of our life, let us improve the colours of our surroundings, let us improve the colours of our elders and juniors and let us improve the colour of the various forms of nature which help keep us alive on this planet. We will, in doing so, improve the colour of the universe and make the Earth believe it should continue to live and not kill itself over a while. Let us not poison the very thing that provides us with a platform to live on.

Similarly, within ourselves also, we have all the colours, but if we look at it from a distance, we find that everything is black and white. If we were to improve our inner colours, our outer colour would be much more radiant and we would also shine within our solar system."

Harrod asked, "Guruji, what about our solar system?"

Guruji replied, "Just as our earth has a solar system where there is a central sun providing radiance to all of us and there are planets, stars and satellites to support its cause, likewise each individual or living species has its solar system. The individual is bound within its solar system. It is for us to understand who or what comprises our solar system, which is the sun for us, who are the planets and who are the satellites and the stars for us. We represent the Earth. Even if we stray into others constellations, we should always keep the roots of our system in place. If we cannot do this, our solar system is going to collapse. There will be shooting stars, meteor showers and also breaking stars and they will come and go. We always feel these broken meteors would strike us and so we keep on taking measures to avoid it, but in the process, we come in its way and get affected by it. What we need to do is, not come in their way at all and we will find ourselves safe."

"Harrod," Guruji said, "You must know by now that what you are being taught by the fishes at the temple, is, but a fragment of what the greater knowledge is, but it is also essential for you to keep learning these facts to recognize the true nature of our existence. It is the layer of cream which forms the basis of our existence and the rest must be there for the cream to be formed."

With this Guruji called off his meeting with Harrod for the day and left Harrod with an unimaginable new insight.

THE SOLUTION TO TERROR

14

That night Harrod wrote whatever he had learnt from Guruji in his diary. After some time, he got up and walked outside his cottage in the cool breezy night. He somehow felt disturbed. His thoughts swam through to the various innocent killings that were taking place in the world and disturbing world peace. At some places, the terrorists were killing and other places, professional killer groups, while yet at other places, it was the local people getting killed, and in the households were the people in the family themselves by infighting. Some killed because of the system of casteism, some because of the rigidness of religion, some for personal egos, some for racial issues, some for land or wealth and some for survival. But the mass killings were happening because of the terrorists, as we called them. His mind was going through all this and his thoughts kept on wandering in the darkness towards the entire world that he had either travelled or read about. The entire world encircled Harrod's head like a practical globe. In every place, there were certain problems, and the problems were growing by the numbers. After about an hour outside, he came back to his cottage, but he had recurring thoughts which he could not keep enslaved in his mind. So, he set about writing them.

God Forbid

Trained in the background

Have taken up their fangs,

And out have come

The deadly snakes of hell.

No sentiments,

No beliefs ever-

Of the mighty God;

Have they just

Come out from their den,

Into the open,

To poison the mortal beings?

The sinners, they killed,

The innocent they slaughtered.

Obsessed the peace of many minds,

Created terror in everybody's eyes;

Frightened a lot,

And, in the ambience,

Made the mortal beings

Go through sleepless nights.

They were preposterous

At their behaviour

This everybody came to know.

But for whom?

Was the hatred,

No one knew.

The streets have been empty,

The doors of houses closed.

The earth, they have terrified,

The souls have become petrified;

But still the challenge,

Has been taken,

Against these

Deadly snakes of hell.

They have poisoned a lot,

They have been cut a lot,

But still, they grow in number,

To create dread, after all.

When this fight will be over

No one knows;

But we just hope!

That these deadly snakes

Will stop their maniacal behaviour,

Understand the misery

Through their sceptical minds,

And surrender themselves,

To the onslaughts of time.

He wanted his message to travel down to every individual living in the world. So, he wrote at length. He knew there was a solution, but it was not by wiping out the races, ostracizing them or jailing them. It had to be something greater. His thoughts were automatically finding the right lines in his diary. He kept writing.

It is a good beginning if the religious or government systems adopt measures such as ostracizing these people from their very own society, for which these people say, they are fighting. But they would not do so, as they know by doing this, they would discourage other members of the same religion. They would be afraid of doing so, fearing the backlash from the people of their religion for taking such measures. For humans, the power seat of any organisation is very important and they will do nothing to disrupt it. All the religious leaders are part of this powerful business just like the politicians who would not enact a law, which later on, can be detrimental to their very own survival. It would require sheer guts.

People, who we term as terrorists, have their groups and even though their groups are condemned by religious sects from time to time, there is no effect on them. They have forced people into terrorism in the name of religion. A terrorist is always going to be a part of the group which will continue to mislead him or her to further their cause. We should not make religion govern people and governments. Religion should only show people the correct path.

Harrod was arriving at a solution. What we need to do is provide a super boost to the ECONOMICAL ADVANCEMENT OF THE NATION & CREATION OF HAPPY MOMENTS for the people, which the terrorists cannot counter or explain, why on earth are they following the cause that their leaders are after. We should help them re-engineer their mindsets about being the ones who can change the livelihood of people and make survival economical and social order possible for them through their acts. The present governments of all countries, for their safe living, continue to support measures such as aiding other groups to create destruction for others. We should make them aware that they will at one point be the targets of the same groups whom they are harbouring, as it is already happening in various countries today.

So, to prevent any mishap in the future, the present governments only could adopt the best solutions. This could happen only when the policies of governments across the world, especially those with greater powers and those who are hungry for the same, are made cleaner, stricter and directed towards thinking positive for ourselves and others. To be happy, we need to shed the hunger for power and move towards the overall well-being and happiness of the people. It is a long exercise and will require an educational revolution along with the Sarva Shiksha Abhiyan (mission of education for all) as in India so that people in the next generation can take steps to rectify this anomaly. Harrod had heard about this mission which India was pursuing when he had come to India for the first time, and he felt that this mission was something that could save us from ignorance and lack of knowledge.

He kept writing. "Just as there are summits by nations by WHO, WTO and other world organisations, there should be equivalent summits to raise the world's educational level, not in terms of technology but to bring about a shift in thinking patterns for masses across the world. There should be NGO's working not just for bringing people above poverty levels and other social causes that they are into but to create an awareness of the greatness of the life that we have got. Once the greatness and the importance of life will be understood by all, they would automatically want to shift and become learned themselves, and learning the correct path would be the most important part of this exercise.

Harrod hoped that people across the world adopted a system of correct education so that they all could decipher the right path for moving ahead for themselves and the future generations.

Once he had noted his thoughts, Harrod felt his mission accomplished for the day. He dozed off into a peaceful slumber.

But that day Harrod had learnt something more meaningful. He had learnt another lesson on connectivity and integration through his recurring thoughts. He had learnt that whatever be the situation, the world cannot be a one-sided platform. For every good, there has been an evil side or else the world will have nothing to progress upon. There is a common linkage between every activity that takes place on this earth. What is bad today for someone, may turn out to be good for the same person in the future? But the person needs to understand this when such an incidence takes place. The core of every transaction results from our very own consciousness, connections and interactions with our families, friends, and acquaintances. It is for us to identify the positive connections in our lives to further our cause.

RELEVANCE OF POSITIVE ATTITUDE

15

Harrod woke up early the next morning. His internal thought process was changing quickly. He had never imagined that meeting Guruji would be a turning point in his life. The world called this a choice of career, but Harrod called it his life. He was young, intelligent, patient and a good listener which made him more responsive to the teachings of Guruji.

Every day, after his observations at the temple, Harrod would wait impatiently for Guruji in the evening. That evening, too, he had waited for Guruji to come and shower his knowledge and blessings on him. Guruji arrived in the garden and asked Harrod to sit in front of him. Harrod obeyed and sat down in the lotus position with both his palms joined in front, in the "namaste" posture.

Guruji spoke at length once again.

"Harrod", Guruji said, continuing on his earlier sermon.

Guruji's voice was very pleasant, soothing and yet with a significant amount of depth. When he spoke, it seemed as if a million waves of the oceans were lashing against the shores; as if the cool breeze was blowing down the mountains; it was as though the clouds were raining incessantly; as if the sun was providing its eternal light with thousands of colours and as if white pearls were falling and bouncing from everywhere. It was an experience beyond imagination.

Guruji said, "You have seen and observed the bowl every day and day by day your knowledge is growing. Just as I had pointed out, if you have observed well, you will have noted that the fishes are moving around the entire day in the small bowl. They teach us to live our lives in the same manner. We are all made of matter, which can be used by us constantly. There is no time for us to rest. We are fortunate to be among the living species of this world and can sleep if we get tired. But imagine, if our planet earth thought about sleeping or dozing off! What would happen if this occurred? At every moment we could have many seasonal changes, would have no track of time and therefore no idea how we can control things. Our life would be deranged, and possibly we would not be living here in this world.

But the fishes teach us to be lively, to keep on moving. If the fishes lost their liveliness for some time, they would die too. Can you imagine water in this world without the fishes? The liveliness of water would be lost if the fishes were not there. From where would the colours be imparted in the vast oceans, seas, rivers, lakes and ponds? The fishes are the life of water.

The fishes are lively throughout the day, as they have a positive attitude. If you tease them, they will play with you, if you pose danger- they will back off, but at the end of it all, once these activities are over, they will return to their normal stature and keep on swimming as if nothing had happened. It is the attitude of the fishes that is very important in life. They forget every incident quick and get back to their normal life as though nothing had happened.

We all must learn to be lively in our personal lives with a positive attitude and must all look towards the achievement of the positive. We must also forget the daily cribbing, forget that someone had insulted, forget the fights, forget the facts of caste, creed and religion, forget personal ego's, forget expectations, but learn to forget and forgive and get back to our daily lives. All of us need to devise a system within ourselves, which could automatically switch off as soon as a negative thought pervades. Negativity is the factor that teaches us to become positive.

The fishes also teach us to become more confident. They teach us to overpower nature and reach its depths and to understand, no matter what nature has in store for us, we can swim through and get back to where we were. They teach us to become more and more confident while tackling the hurdles that life has posed for us. If we lose confidence today, we will shatter our tomorrow and our life will become dark. Just as the fishes overcome whatever fights they undergo in their lives; we too must learn to light up our lives at every corner of darkness.

The fishes also teach us that the big and the small can co-exist together. If you have observed, there are 4 slightly larger goldfishes and 2 smaller black ones in the bowl. But each one experiments with the other inside the bowl. Sometimes it is the small black fishes that are chasing the larger goldfishes and at other times, it is the goldfishes chasing the black fishes. They keep on playing throughout the day without fighting.

The fishes, as you have observed, play with no knowledge of caste, creed, religion or colour. They know not that there is a difference between the two colours and sizes. It is the knowledge that we have gained over some time and the greed of using that knowledge to our advantage that has taken the form of caste, creed, religion or racism.

We brought religion to lay down rules so that we do not go astray. But some people have taken the support of religion to become power centres for ruling others, which is not the right purpose. The fishes do not know about any religion, but they all know that there is an external force that keeps them going.

The fishes also teach us the wonder that nature has provided us with. We are all part of this great nature, and we should see that we preserve it in its natural form.

Look at what all the fishes can teach us"

It was getting dark now, so Guruji stood and went away a bit earlier than usual. Three days back Harrod had made small observations, on which Guruji was continuing to light him up. It was a wonder and Harrod could see that, though he thought he had observed the fishes well, there was always something new in his finding and so was Guruji's sermon to him.

Harrod still did not know what would happen once the process of observing the fishes would be over, and he did not think about this aspect now. He preferred to stay in the present. But this time would come soon. How soon would only depend on what Harrod would observe next?

Based on whatever he had learnt from Guruji, that night Harrod penned in his diary:

The Truth

It is a whirlpool,

Where we all

Seem to revolve inadvertently;

Where the suction power,

Pulls us

Deeper and deeper,

Into a place,

Which is grappled

By different predicaments;

Where all

Our courage and confidence

Seem to melt.

But still!

The world keeps afloat,

With those-

That swim through

With determination,

And will power,

To be ultimately led

To utter success.

LOVE IS CENTRAL

16

During the past 2 days, Guruji had given various sermons to Harrod. He had also made some more observations of the fishes which he could not tell Guruji about, so he was eager to share this too.

So that evening, Harrod told Guruji about his last two days' observation as well. Each day the observations were getting deeper and Harrod had got completely immersed into them. Every day, he would wait for the morning and then for the evening so that Guruji could explain the significance of his observation. But the last two days had been slightly different.

During the past two days, Harrod's first observation was:

When he went near the bowl one fine morning, he observed the fishes were recognizing him. He could see them lash in the water, wriggle and become very impatient as soon as he approached them. This was quite unusual for him. How could there be a connection between him and the fishes, where they could become a part of his life?

His second observation was:

When Harrod moved his hand next to the bowl, the fishes would respond by going backwards and forwards.

His third observation was:

If he moved his hand away, the fishes would come searching next to the glass for him.

"Guruji, what does all this mean?" asked Harrod. "I can understand that being a living being, as a reflex action, they are reacting to my action. But is it something more than this?" Harrod asked.

Guruji explained. "Harrod what you have observed is quite scientific, and you have explained that through reflex actions. But what was this science? Much before we started recognizing science, these things were ingrained into our very own bodies. We are a part of science ourselves. We have been given the gift of emotions such as crying, laughing, getting angry, becoming sad and many more and one of the best emotions given to us is that of love.

Love is something that has taught us how to live this life. In all the three observations that you have made, there is one common emotion, the emotion of love. You have been going near the fish every day for the past fourteen days, and now there is a common bonding between the fishes and you. No amount of science can explain this to you. They recognize you, and they are not afraid of you anymore. They get eager to meet you when you go close to them. Somehow, their biological clocks tell them that at a particular time you will visit them. They have their alarm systems and know that you are going to feed them at a particular time and they want to play with you as well. They are not aware that your purpose of going there is just to make observations and then understand why they do the things they do. But in the last few days, they have understood you and you too have got some connection with them. Just as they expect you to visit them every day, you are eager to visit them every morning too.

So, there is a bond, the bond of Love. That you become eager to visit them is an offshoot of love. Love is something unique, which people, animals, plants and all other living forms recognize. They all know where there is love, they will also respond by showing reciprocal love.

Harrod, you must have observed that when you take your fingers or your hands closer to the bowl, the fishes come near you and then when you get very closer; they move back. There is a wireless connection of love between the two of you. You may not know, but we are all connected. It is just when you get near certain people or objects that you realize this. Consciously we are so lost in our day to day lives that we cannot understand the significance of getting in touch with one another. Every person meets another for some destined purpose, which he understands when the right time comes.

You must have also observed that the fishes continue to live happily within themselves and this is also due to love, till the common factor - food is given to them. But if they could share it between themselves without a hitch, no one would go hungry and there would not be a fight between any of them. Being fishes they can afford to do so. However, being humans, we can't and being the most intelligent species, we should still learn from them and share and love to avoid fights, to avoid hunger, to avoid lust, to avoid every other misfortune that life could bring to us.

Love is something that a child recognizes when he or she is born. The child recognizes where he can find love and will always move in that direction. We must all learn from our childhood actions. We must all learn to rewind our childhood to understand the fact of love and you find that the more you unwind, the more you will understand its relevance in your life and the life of every other person who has mattered or will matter to you from now on.

That we met is connected by the simple string of love. We may convert love to hatred by our actions, but if we analyse it closely, we find that love is the single factor by which any meeting can succeed. Love is eternal, love is God, and love is the basis of life. You must learn to love everyone that comes across you, and soon you will find the same love coming back to you in different forms."

That day Harrod realized his sudden meeting with Guruji and getting accepted by him with little effort. Harrod thought about his daily meetings with the fishes; he thought of his acquaintances, his friends, his family, his parents, his society and how he was related to all of them. He was tied to everybody by a very thin cord which could break anytime if he pulled it hard. But till the time the cord was being pulled with little pressure, no one could break the relationship between any of them. He could now see vividly that everyone who mattered to him was smiling for him and as they were being recalled in his thoughts. This was something that every mentor or Guru had taught his disciple.

Harrod's inner mind was brimming with smiles, and the warmth was touching his soul by now. He did not know how to express it, as only his body could feel the solemn vibrations.

That night Harrod wrote some of the most beautiful words he could think about. Every word came from his heart. He wrote:

The Passage

Silent is the love,

That rings in the life

Of many mortal minds.

The opulent and the paupers;

The lanky and the rotund;

The proletariat and petit-bourgeois;

The amiable and the morose;

The sagacious;

The fortunate and unfortunate ones,

All share

This most bewildering time.

It speaks to itself,

Becomes happy and smiles

In its limpid brainy ocean-

Till miles.

It is a crescendo of feelings

In the scrupulous mind,

And there is no catharsis

To supplement-

This inexplicable inner mind.

The kin nor the crony,

Come to know

Of this extreme joy-

As there is no chronicle

For this passage of time.

God –

Has been magnanimous

To all humankind.

Harrod knew that through his writings, he could get across his message to the entire world. What he could not do in a single day to the entire world, he could get it across in this way. The message in his diary was getting bigger, and so was his knowledge with time at the ashram.

MAKE THE WORLD A BETTER PLACE

17

The following day when Harrod went to the temple, he tried very hard to identify some fresh activities of the fishes. However hard he tried; he could find nothing new. His thinking capability was drying up and his mind had got blocked. It was as if his observation had come to a standstill. But he knew also that, till Guruji wanted him to learn, there would surely be messages from the fishes for him. It was like getting continuous letters till one responded to it - a constant reminder that we must read the messages. After concentrating for an hour, he finally left the temple dejected as he could not decipher any fresh activity or learning for himself that morning.

In the evening, when Harrod met Guruji, he told him, "Guruji, I couldn't identify anything new today. I just saw the fishes swimming through and through, and that's it. I do not know what that means, but that's what I saw and I do not think that there was anything else there to know."

Guruji looked at Harrod, and once again put on his charismatic, soft smile.

He explained, "Harrod, today you have seen the same thing that you have seen daily. But in it lies the great truth. The truth of continuing to walk through in your life, no matter what comes your way - whether it be something good or evil in your life, something sweet or sour."

Harrod asked, "But Guruji, with what I have seen today, how come the fishes teach us this?

Guruji explained, "Today, you saw the fishes swim through and through and did you notice any of them resting?"

Harrod said, "No, Guruji, none of them rested even a single minute. Sometimes the fishes would stop, but their fins continued to work for them, so they could remain static inside the water."

"Well then," Guruji said, "You see what I mean. The fishes do not know what is resting. They will become stationary, but will not rest as we do. The slightest of disturbance will make them move forward. We must learn from this that we have not been created to rest, but to continue to do the work destined for us. We must keep on working and thinking for the betterment of society and the planet. Our society is not just the people with whom we live but it is everyone who is in touch with us and even those who are unknown to us. The fishes do not know what society is and probably that what keeps them working on their way in life continuously."

Was Guruji again hinting at something? Harrod thought.

Guruji continued, "We have created our societies and we always want to be bound within it. Just imagine what would happen if we were to expand beyond it, without thinking about the consequences. Do you think there would be chaos or amity?"

Harrod thought for a while and then said, "I think if we were to bring everything and everyone in the world into one society, there would be amity because when we create our societies, we do it to get everyone's love and appreciation and bring together a common thought process. So, if the length and breadth were indeed expanded, all these factors would be greater. But then, why do we fear a backlash within our society when we do something different?"

Guruji replied, "Harrod, in a society there are common thoughts and ways of doing things created over time. We have made these and we define them thinking these to be the best. Over time, the ways of doing things get ingrained into the coming generations and they think it to be the gospel truth. Any difference is always challenged. So, when there is any difference of thought or opinion, there is an uprising.

But you will also notice if the difference is great and determined, then there will be positive changes and then society will adopt it, eventually."

Coming back to his earlier thoughts, Guruji said, "Have you ever thought about the fishes? What would happen if, just like the nights, we were to stop working during the daytime also? Remember, if we do not exert, then we can work twenty-four hours. But if we exert while working continuously, our bodies would break down. It is always good to pause and recharge.

If we were to see a machine that has not been used for some time, there would be deposits of rust at different places and when we try to restart the machine, it will start but with slightly greater pressure after applying some oil and servicing it. But if the machine lies idle for some more time, then the whole machine becomes so rusty and ceases to work that we have to scrap it. Similar is our body machine and the more we use it, the smoother it gets. The less we use it, the greater will be our inability to find success.

We, humans, have our very own machine working twenty-four hours for us. We are free to use it as we want. This freedom has been provided to us. What we do is our very own business. Some people work very hard throughout their lives and in the process create new things benefitting the world. These are people who use their human-machine to their maximum advantage. Then other people lie down, doing nothing in their lives. These people get rusted over time and are scrapped over time by society or get scrapped themselves through poverty, diseases, stress and death. Then again, some people live their lives by working for some time and remaining idle for the remaining part. These are people who live only for themselves and do no good for this world. Again, some people give up their living for spiritual purposes in search of God. These people come to teach the world about the theory of God and how people can come closer to this divine truth. Although by their acts they show people how to follow some spiritual path in life, yet they cannot show them their true purpose of taking birth on this planet, which is to continue living their life to its full potential. The mantras, the prayers, the teachings, the lessons, are meant to attain our full potential and we need not get engrossed in it completely. They teach us to keep our lives happy without material fulfilment, but nowhere do they tell us not to keep working for the benefit of this world.

Be it day or night, we can always do something for the benefit of this world. Let us all think of how we can teach this world to make it a better place to live in. As I already told you earlier, every person has got a specific purpose in life and it is for us to realize what the same is and keep working towards it, till we achieve it. Once that purpose is achieved, you will find a new purpose has been created for you. But putting ourselves to rest is not the solution to any of our purposes.

Resting is something every human does when his/her mind tells him that his body can't take the pressures any longer. It is an excuse that we build to overcome our deficiencies. Some people find success in their respective fields and they rest less than six hours a day, but there are very few people who find genuine success by resting over six hours a day."

"But Guruji," Harrod interrupted. "There are people who say that their destiny is fixed and no one can do anything about it. Some people only believe in astrological sciences and when they find themselves not succeeding in life because of the planetary positions they are into, they say, why should they work, if destiny does not want them to? Will these people ever succeed in life?"

Guruji explained, "Harrod, every person's destiny is fixed. But we will speak about it on another day. The time is not yet come for you to understand the actual significance of destiny. The temple will teach you.

But I have been destined to teach this world the right path, you for the moment have been destined to learn from me. Come to think about it and you will see there are people destined to fight for their countries throughout their lives, people who will protect their countries' borders, people who are destined to live a poverty-ridden life, people who are destined to live a healthy & wealthy life, people who are destined to invent new things in life and a lot of other people who are destined to other forms of living.

But that does not mean that the rich should not keep working or the poor should not work for the betterment of his life or his world at large. Given the true nature of humans, we will become lazy if our destinies are revealed. We will give our way of life to be what is destined. The future of anybody is very enticing and everyone wants to know about what the future beholds for him. Yet, we cannot identify the true potential within us, even if the brightest futures were told to us. The future of the past is today and today will be tomorrow. There are scripts written within our body and everything is defined in the scripts within us. We can change our scripts, but that will take long years of self-realization, which again will take a lot of hard work on our part for changing our mind and believe me, people who can do this cannot rest at all, leave aside 6 hours. Their minds will keep on working, even if their bodies stop to work.

So, be it the fishes whom you saw today or any other living form on this earth or universe, we are all born to keep working our ways throughout our lives. When we work, we find that the surrounding universe is unfurling itself. The surrounding space becomes much cleaner and clearer. There will be a vacuum created for us where we can travel with no hitch. The vacuum takes away all kinds of fissures and frictions in our lives, and we walk on and on into an unending horizon."

Guruji left with these words for the day.

During that whole evening, one sentence from Guruji kept Harrod disturbed, which was about destiny being fixed. Harrod, being a commoner, knew about soldiers fighting and sacrificing their lives. The soldiers would work day and night for the safety of their nation. They had all joined to defend their countries, even though they knew that survival would be a tough choice for them while serving their country. He had seen soldiers from his country being sent on different missions to different parts of the world, and it would make him wonder about their mindset and their might to overcome the fear of dying. According to Harrod, death was the greatest fear of all. All other fears ultimately led to this fear somehow.

But Harrod also knew that the thought which he was experiencing at that moment, was there again to teach him something, just like the fishes. Each thought that Harrod had every evening after Guruji's learned discourse, were a source of learning for him.

Thoughts flowed like a cascade through Harrod's mind once again and he wrote:

In the Glory

The daredevil soldier

Marched up the mighty mountains,

Walked through unending plains,

Fought through

The devastating deserts,

Went to the darkest

Depths of the oceans,

Guarded the borders

Like huge mountain barriers,

Saluted before the flag,

And sang its glory.

All these for whom?

All this for the love

For the nation's people.

To protect them

Against the selfish enemies.

Now his term is completed.

He no more has

The strength to stand up.

And then,

What does he get in return?

The cognomen of a soldier!

Which is washed out

From the sickly brains

Of the People!

He is now incarcerated in the midst

Of all those great mountains,

Deserts, plains and oceans,

Where once he lived

For the love of his nation.

But today to survive himself.

It was true that they were destined to serve their countries, and it was also true that they took it bravely and no one cared for them once their service was over. Harrod sat down with his legs and arms folded and prayed for the well-being of all the soldiers around the world.

Even though in reality it was difficult, Harrod thought about a united world, a world with no malice towards anyone, a world where there was no need for any soldier to fight amongst themselves, a world where every person was fighting for the survival of others, a world where everyone worked for the well-being of others, a world where every person saw a reason to smile, a world where every person worked and worked and worked just like the fishes who kept swimming and swimming and swimming, but still smiled at him when he came near them.

SOMETIMES DISABILITY MAKES ONE STRONGER

18

Harrod did not know how long the exercise of observing the fishes in the bowl would last, but he did not care about it any longer. He was learning new things from them which no one else could have taught him. With time, he was yearning to learn more and more, and the meaning of living a meaningful life was getting clearer to him, day by day.

The next day, Harrod was up again at four-thirty in the morning and he finished his morning chores as usual. Just after this, as he was going to the temple, he saw a person who seemed to be a temple devotee, spray cool water on the plants. This fascinated him as the person was walking with a stick in one hand and a water sprayer in the other. Harrod went closer to him and kept trailing him keeping a safe distance. What Harrod could not understand was that this person was walking slowly, checking every plant with his hands and then spraying water on it. Harrod could not understand why this phenomenon continued with every plant that came on the man's way. Getting closer to him, he examined the person minutely. He saw that even though the person's eyes were wide open, and he was seeing everything, yet; he was examining every plant before watering it.

Harrod stopped the person and asked him the reason.

The devotee explained, "Sir, it is my duty to water the plants every morning. But I cannot see the colourful world as I am blind. Since I cannot see, I must examine every plant before watering it. This is important, as I must know where and what I am watering. I have to perform the job assigned to me with due diligence. I feel a sense of satisfaction when I have watered every plant properly."

Harrod was taken aback. He had not thought for a moment that the person was blind, as he had seen the devotees' eyes wide open. Harrod apologized to him promptly and left the person to keep watering the plants as usual. But the thought of a person not being able to see and still being so thoughtful kept on bothering him. He had seen many blind people during his life, but little had he ever imagined their plight.

He, however, continued as usual to the temple for his daily lessons. When he reached the temple, the bowl, as usual, lay in the middle of the room and the fishes inside it. As he approached them, the fishes wriggled and wrangled and seemed as though they were dancing, as if it thrilled them when they saw him come near. Harrod took his hand near the bowl and the fishes withdrew. He took his hand away, and the fishes came near. Again, he took his hand near and the fishes withdrew and when he took his hand away; the fishes came near. Harrod felt thrilled at this game. He had heard of dolphins play with people but had never thought that these small fishes would play with him in this way. It was unusual behaviour for him to see. The whole incident was so exciting. It pulled Harrod closer to the fishes. The fishes recognized him somehow, and he also saw that as the fishes danced the plants nearby also swayed. It felt as though the plants were also enjoying the show. He remembered what Guruji had told him two days back.

Throughout the entire hour that Harrod was there at the temple, he played with the fishes and the fishes also reciprocated by playing with him. It was so much fun, and Harrod enjoyed it thoroughly.

When Harrod narrated this minor incident to Guruji in the evening, he explained:

"Harrod, as I told you earlier, although you have played with the fishes and they with you, the significance of this is much greater. If you were to think rationally, you find that the fishes have once again taught you an important function of life.

As I told you earlier, there is a wireless connection between every living organism in this world, between you and the earth and between you and the universe. The systems have been constructed so beautifully that you will have to recognize and appreciate its finesse. The fishes would not have recognized you if there was no connection. People will tell you it is a reflex action and they are not wrong. But that they come and go back suggests that there is a connection. There is a common cord between the two of you. You must have also seen that it was only one or two fishes that come and play with you and not all. Why not rest? It is only because these one or two are connected with you closely. The rest will react when there is another person who unlike you but has his connections fixed with them or emanates similar energy. They will react only when there is a connection.

This is the supreme power of recognition between all of us. It is only because of this special wireless connection that we are recognized by some people and not everyone. Even in the recognition process, we find that of the few people who do, some are deeply connected while others are not so.

When you move around in the streets, you will find many people but not all will recognize you. You will find most of the people who pass by, will not even look at you. There will be a few who will look at you and still pass by. Still, there will be others who will look and smile at you, and then there are few others who will smile and acknowledge your existence on this earth. This can be true for any gender. And the few who acknowledge you will be the ones whom you will remember. The ones who have smiled at you will be remembered by you for a brief period. The rest will simply be wiped out from the memory of your conscious mind. But here also your subconscious mind is at work and every single thing that your eyes would have seen consciously or unconsciously is recorded on its memory for an infinite time.

Beyond the power of recognition is the power of interaction. The fishes that have interacted with you are the fishes that will always do so till there is some adverse energy that makes them move away, while others are not concerned at all. We find the same things between people of different cultures, races, creed and religions. There is an interaction between the two kinds whenever there is a common vibrancy between the two. These two kinds will have a common connection which only these two will acknowledge and know. Every time they interact, there will always be positive vibes or energy oozing out between them. It will create a positive environment between the two which is the most essential part of living. For any eventful interaction, the working of positive energies is most essential.

Thus, the power of recognition and interaction is very important if one needs to progress in life. If you can have a positive environment surrounding you always, then you find that there will be a lot of connectivity between you and anybody else and when there will be connectivity-people, plants, animals, fishes, will interact with you with much more vigour. With people, you will understand this vital aspect, but with the others, you will have to put your entire mind together to understand this connectivity. But once you have recognized this, you will find everything will dance and sing to your tune.

Another important point here, is, even if you can make others sing and dance to your tune, you must not misuse this divine power, as, when you do, the positive energies will turn negative and it will backfire on you.

Thus, it is important to understand the meaning of the closeness of the fishes with you. Tomorrow you will once again understand this aspect and the bond will get stronger and closer. Over time, this bonding will get stronger and more perfect.

With the physical world outside, you find that the more you use the existing resources, the more they diminish and get weaker. But with the world that has been created within us, the more you use it, the stronger the bonds will get, the stronger the wiring will get and the stronger will be the connectivity."

Guruji got up and left Harrod to think deeper.

It was yet another day of revelation for Harrod. He longed to go back to the fishes and enjoy with them once again. He had now received a good reason to be with them. They were like pets to him. He remembered people having pets such as dogs, cats, horses, squirrels, snakes, and caterpillars etc. He was now able to understand the strange connection being established between the pet owners and their pets.

Although the thought of going back the next morning to the fishes was getting Harrod excited, he was still feeling disturbed and his thoughts were rushing back to the morning hours wherein he had seen the blind man and had experienced his connection with the world outside him. In the moonlight, he sat down outside his cottage and imagined how the blind people lived their life. He could see that life had given different disabilities to different people, and each one treated them differently. Each disability had a certain degree attached to it, and their actions ruled the degrees either in this life or later. As his thoughts swayed, he wrote:

The New World

The world he saw,

And

He saw it,

For the last time.

He cried sobbed, wailed,

But

Ne'er could see.

The world hath changed,

His life became deranged.

Now,

There was a question,

What would be his next action?

He had seen the World,

Bright, colourful, beautiful,

And,

Full of life,

With himself

A part of it.

His thoughts were shattered;

To other people

It couldn't have mattered.

But,

He had to live on,

Generate his inner powers,

And not be subject to

Lord's blessed showers.

Only then,

Could he see the world?

With a different perspective,

As he had never seen before.

It was not just the case of blind people, but other people were also disabled in different forms. Not just people, but there were many animals, birds, insects who lived their lives with different disabilities. Harrod sat down, folded his legs and prayed to God to relieve each one from their sufferings and also to teach him ways of healing people who were suffering from these kinds of ailments. He thought about himself as being one of the lucky few who did not have any of it, but who also knew, why, when, where and how one could get affected and get disabled for life. Destiny was supreme.

Within this incidence, Harrod had learnt his next lesson. Everything on this earth is connected. Within oneself also, every part is integrated and we cannot function perfectly with any of them missing. These parts offer the connection between individuals, the world, and the universe. Without the body's system itself, there could be no connection at all.

The occurrence of such coincidences was a part of the ashram plan and they were a part of what Guruji had planned for Harrod as well. These incidences were also teaching Harrod truths the fishes could not narrate but had its relevance in the day-to-day lives of organisms living on Mother Earth. Harrod still had to learn the basic truth of living.

THIS IS EVERYONE'S DESTINY

19

Over time, the same activities continued and then one day, while Harrod concentrated on the fishbowl to find some new activity, he observed there was something amiss in the bowl. He quickly got up and looked at it closely. At first, he didn't know what had happened. Then, on focusing a bit more, he saw one of the black fishes lay at the bottom of the bowl and other fishes were trying to poke and shake it. But the black one at the bottom would not budge. Harrod instantly knew that this fish was dead. It was the end of its life. Birth and death were a way of life, and by now Harrod was aware of this very well. He read daily in the newspapers about the deaths that took place and the different ways in which people met with their fate. Not just death, but he had also read about the different circumstances in which babies were born and their different places of birth.

He had to do something, quick. He got up, got the small fish net and hauled up the dead fish. There was no life, so even when he got the fish out of the water, there was no reaction from it. Although the fishes were Harrod's teachers, this one had to be taken out of the bowl and kept away from the other fishes as it had lost the ability to teach anyone, any more and it would only pollute the water if it was kept there. Harrod took out the blackfish and carried it to the drain outside and put it there. The water in the drain would take care of the dead fish. If there was any bigger fish, it could not have fitted in the drain and so would have to be put somewhere else. Harrod could bury it. He had seen the other fishes become perturbed by the dead fish. He was not feeling too good about the loss of one of his favourite fishes. They had all become a part of his life.

It perturbed Harrod. He went near the bowl and decided to clean the bowl and provide fresh water to the fishes. But before he could do this, he took the permission of Guruji. In the process, he also thought if the fishes would remember any of the incidents that had just occurred. This was the first time he was changing the water in the bowl.

That evening, Harrod narrated the entire incident to Guruji. Although Guruji knew about the dead fish, as he had himself permitted changing of the water, Harrod still wanted him to know about the entire incident.

When Harrod stopped, Guruji said, "Harrod, have you now learnt the meaning of destiny."

Harrod asked, "Guruji, how's the death of the fish related to destiny", and sure enough Harrod got the answer.

Guruji said, "Harrod, DEATH is the ultimate destiny of everyone on this earth. Whatever destinies come your way during your life; the destiny of death overpowers every other destiny. Every person or living thing born in this universe must face this destiny, whether early or late. The fish you just saw had lived its life and met its destiny. So, will you, me and everyone else here and outside this place, this country, this world. That is how the complete system works. No one can escape death, and no one can explain our birth or our existence on earth.

With every death, there is another birth and this cycle will not stop till we don't put an end to this by fully enacting our part well during this life. This is the law of Karma. Harrod, you have reached the last phase of the first cycle of taking your lessons here. The temple of destiny teaches what you have just learnt. Whatever you have done during your lifetime will ultimately come to an end. Destiny is decided.

During your last few days here, you have learnt about love, hate, patience, confidence, positive attitudes, power, force, a reason to smile and various other facets of life which help determine the ultimate destiny of every person. All these factors are very important in this part of life. But death will bring everything to an end. All these things that play their part during life come to an end here.

You must be thinking, if death is the destiny of all the factors, then why go after doing good only during this life? Why not enjoy the bad things also; after all, you only have this life to go through and enjoy every aspect, whether good or evil?

The answer to this question is, life does not end here. It goes beyond saying that all the facets which you have become a part of, in this life, will annotate your further forms in this world. There are forms of life beyond your present life. Your soul will continue to develop till you can prove to your desired system that you should not and cannot develop any longer. Then you reach the stage of salvation where your soul will get absorbed into infinity.

If you have seen in the life that surrounds you, just to name a few kinds of bad habits, some people would smoke, drink and take drugs to boost their self-confidence. They all do these to boost their ego and to satisfy their shattered self-confidence. However, over time they become addicted to its effects. Once they are addicted, these things become a part of their system. Now if you observe properly, you find they will get back the results as sufferings for these wrongful acts performed during their lifetime, either at the time of their youth or the end of their life. If they get it back during their prime time, then it means that life has provided them with a chance or opportunity to correct themselves. But if they get it during their old age, when they are going to die, it means that the painful suffering is for wrong activities which the person did and did not care or repent for, during his life.

Nature has provided everyone in this system with opportunities abound for correcting themselves, but we must know and understand when we have done wrong to correct it. We must listen to our inner voice.

Goodness is the part that keeps us in this line of activity. It is the positive energy with all its outstanding characteristics that change your inner world's programming into recognizing your true self, which will relieve your soul of continuous transformations or recreations.

Death only determines that your current life form is over and you should get prepared to face other forms that are destined for you. Since we all are inter-connected with ourselves, this world and the universe, it is but natural that the universe is also our world and not just this planet earth. While the people of this planet are happy to conquer space physically, we can travel infinitely into space without physically going there. Our mind is supreme and we can do whatever we want to do with it.

But coming back, death will supersede any of the activities formed within the walls of our mind, and it is the single largest factor that can stop its functioning. With death, we will ultimately unite with the universal truth."

Guruji's words had struck the right chords. Harrod knew exactly where he stood. He had now learned what he could have understood long ago if he had focused well on his life's activities. Everything that Guruji had spoken till that day seemed so simple, yet so true. All the aspects were part of his everyday life, and he could have recognized them, anyway. But here was Harrod with Guruji to learn it through the medium of the fishes. He could now understand why the connectivity and integration of every activity was an integral part of everyone and the system.

From what Guruji had told him that day, Harrod had thoughts pouring all over him and he wanted to express it in words. So, he wrote in his diary:

Change

The oblivious darkness.

Then illumination

Into the vistas

Of a new world.

Great metamorphosis,

Then continued

Entanglement and freedom.

After which-

Drooping images,

And the fainting light

Into the supernatural

Third dimensional part;

And ultimate darkness

Rekindles

Into another horizon,

Entirely different.

Harrod had written many articles during his life, but this one was special. It had changed everything in his life. This one explained what life was all about. It was what life would be. He now knew about the significance of darkness before birth and after death. Life itself provided some light to us for a particular time, to enable us to recognize what we have received and given during this lifetime. But after death, this light would form a part of the soul and would determine the soul's ultimate direction. Life is from white to black, while colours are just to fathom it.

LET LIFE CARRY ON

20

After the previous day's interaction with the fishes and as per Guruji's instruction, Harrod had brought in some holy water from the river Ganges and had washed the dead fish with it, before putting it into the drain. This was part of the ritual. The drain would carry the fish to the river and the river to the sea, and at each place, the water would take care of the remains of the fish.

Then Harrod kept the remaining Ganges water next to the bowl of fishes. He now had to change the water of the bowl, but......

For the entire day, that day and the next, Harrod sat next to the bowl watching the remaining fishes. The other fishes seemed lost after the sudden loss of the blackfish. They seemed to have lost their friend and with that, their appetite too. It was all too real to believe. The remaining fishes had gone fasting. All of them stayed at the bottom of the bowl and did not come up to the surface. They stayed there poking their faces where the dead black fish lay during its last breath. They would eat none of their food pills in the morning or the evening and appeared they were mourning the loss of their partner. It was a strange sight.

Harrod had not met Guruji for two complete days now. He could not get over the fact that the fishes were mourning the death of one of their mates. Harrod knew that humans and animals mourned, but fishes? He could have never imagined a similar reaction from them. It was an emotional gathering. A question was disturbing his mind. Did the fishes have emotions too and that too, these small ones?

After two days, however, Guruji himself called Harrod and asked him, "Harrod, how come you have not come to me for the last two days," and Harrod narrated the total story in tears.

Guruji explained, "Harrod, do you see the connection now. The fishes were connected, but so were you with them. Haven't you also lost your sleep along with them? The fishes breathe just like you and me, they feel just like you and me, they see just like you and me. They also have their senses, just like we do.

But, with this, you must learn to be part of the entire system. As I told you earlier, everyone in this world is connected. You must feel for everyone, your heart must be able to ring bells into everyone else's, your mind must be able to work with everyone else's, and your body must be able to gel with everyone else's. It is the inner tune within each one of us, which we must recognize and get connected with.

This is how the world must proceed and progress if we want to make this world a better place to live in."

Guruji continued, "Harrod, you have put in two days of your life's mourning with the fishes. You have seen them become sad and have seen them suffer for two days. You have shared their grief, yet you have done nothing to get them to overcome this grief. If you had come to me during the first day itself, I would have let you know what to do, so that their life would not get affected this way and would continue as usual.

But this was destined for them and you. You had to learn from this and you will.

We all wish life must go on forever, as we are so much connected with it- mentally, physically and emotionally. We always wish that death should not take the place in life, but we cannot shirk away from the truth. The truth is, we must all die one day, and it is also true that life for others must continue as before. We become too emotional for others who become a part of our life, and that's also because it's a part of our laid-out destiny. We have been provided with this extraordinary gift in life. However, we must also learn to control it, we must learn to bring it within our ambit.

Let not your emotions rule over you, but you must learn to rule your emotions. Let the tears roll, but let not the smile vanish. Make death a part of your life and you will enjoy the fruits of life for much greater extents. You will learn the purpose of life if you accept death to be a part of your system. Death clears the way for others, death is the reason people are born, death makes us realize our genuine powers- we can control a lot of things but not death. Death makes us understand that our body and soul are separate. The soul is supreme and pure, but our actions leave marks on it and so it has to undergo different transformations, till it clears all hurdles to emerge in its purest form once again.

Throughout the last few days, you have enjoyed with the fishes and had never thought that one day, death would be the outcome and they would get separated from you. The more you get emotionally involved, the more you will suffer. The more you make them part of your life, the more tears they will make you shed at the end. Tears will roll away, thoughts will continue to torment, but will it help you in any way? With whomsoever you get involved, you must understand that every incident has occurred to teach you something new. If you can understand this, you will understand the reason for the occurrence of the events in your life, and then you will be able to choose the correct path.

When emotions take control, the common thought between all living beings is that they can't do anything during that time, as they do not think with their brains but are compelled to think through their heart. But understand this - our heart is just a term that explains the emotional part of our brain. We can activate any part of our brain, anytime. Different regions in the brain control different activities. The rest of the body is a network of veins, nerves, muscles, tendons, ligaments and bones. All are controlled by the brain and if we can learn to control the mind, we can do whatever we wish except control death. We can extend death through inbuilt controls and external mechanics, but cannot avoid it.

The temple of destiny shows this. You have now learnt the truth and in doing so, have learnt the ways of life as well. After one week, you must go away from this temple and get yourself involved in the second part of the cycle of destiny. For the next few days that you are here, you must take corrective actions for the death of the fish and continue the same activities that you have been doing for so long.

However, on the last day that you will be here, you must come to me at midnight when the world is asleep. I will wait for you in this temple. There is something more important that you must know before you depart from here.

But now to get over this, you must get some water from the river Ganges. We revere this river's water here in this country. Bathe the rest of the fishes and the plants in this water first and then throw away the water. Clean and fill the bowl once again with fresh water from the Ganges. Be careful that we must bring this water from the source of the river Ganges. It is in its purest form there. Then place the fishes and plants back into it. It will clean away all the fish's thoughts and yours. But do this tomorrow morning when you go back to the temple."

With this, Guruji walked away.

That evening once again, Harrod sat on the rocks near his cottage. It was dark all around and thoughts of his youth came back to him. Harrod now compared the plight of the fishes with that of his youth time which he had passed during his life. He knew each person had to go through the difficulties of life before death. In its pursuit, some lose their lives while others swim through it.

Harrod wrote something different that day:

<u>Oh! The Stage</u>

Being in the midst,

Of all those

Friendly gestures,

The juvenile

Surmounts the hill.

Not realizing

The coercion on it

It still climbs on,

To face

The jeopardy of youth.

The embellished,

Stage of youth,

Blown into misused production

And conundrums,

Is not frazzled

In the oblivious excitements.

The venerable youth

Mixed with flabbergasted

Rhetoric

Is hewed ultimately

Into consternation.

Only can the crutch of humanism

Now appear,

To make it convalesce

After the great ordeal;

Away from a destitute

And intimidated condition,

Into a stage

Of relaxed

And frisky life.

WE CREATE OUR ENVIRONMENT

21

Early the next morning, just as Guruji had advised, Harrod brought the water of the river Ganges, which was kept in Guruji's ashram in a separate place. He brought the water in a new pail and kept it on the floor nearby. As he caught hold of the fishbowl to empty it, he realized that the fishes already knew that Harrod was up to catch them. He saw them dash helter-skelter in the bowl. Harrod placed the fishnet inside the bowl.

He wanted to catch the goldfish first. The first goldfish seemed intelligent and slowly learnt that Harrod wanted to put it into another vessel. So, it slowly came into the net by itself and Harrod swiftly put it in the bucket of water without wasting a second. It was now the turn of the next one. The other goldfishes did not want to get caught too. They sensed danger and jumped about. It was a lovely sight. However, Harrod caught them one by one and placed them comfortably in the bucket nearby. It was now the turn of the remaining blackfish. They were smaller than the goldfishes and so took advantage of the round curves of the bowl to avoid getting caught. It easily escaped every time Harrod put the net inside. The net was square, and the bowl had round curves. Harrod's sixth sense triggered inside him. It was now up to Harrod to see how he could get the fishes in the net. He slowly put the net inside and waited. Little by little, the fish overcame the fear of being caught. It came near the net and Harrod gently lifted it out of the bowl and placed it neatly into the bucket. Harrod then took out the plants and placed them in the bucket as well.

Harrod cleaned the fishbowl dexterously and filled it back with the water from the river Ganges. He then cleaned the plants and placed them back inside the bowl. All this time the fishes swam inside the bucket filled with water from the river Ganges, but this time the surroundings were different. They felt alien in the bucket. But still being in the water, they swam around without being aware that they would again be transferred to the glass bowl after the cleaning activity was over.

Once the cleaning was over, it was time for the fishes to be sent back to their original home- the fishbowl.

One by one, Harrod placed all the fishes back into the bowl. The fishes looked happy in the cool, fresh and lucid water. Everything about them looked fresh as if they had a fantastic bath. The fresh look made Harrod understand the charm of freshwater. Water was the sole reason for the survival of these aquatic creatures, and freshwater made them look beautiful.

The fishes felt so fresh, that as soon as Harrod put them in the bowl, it seemed as if they had forgotten the incident which had taken place two days back. The fishes swam with a new life. They felt wonderful. Their colours shone in the bright morning light. Each one of them seemed thrilled. Harrod put in the food pills and each of them ate it. This had not happened during the past two days. But just as Guruji had predicted, this changeover had its desired effect and had them changed once again to their old self.

The whole incident had Harrod shaken. He had received the message. All living species are inter-connected among their clan and also outside their natural environment, and water was a medium that can help wash the miseries of life. The fishes were teaching Harrod some brilliant lessons of life which he had never foreseen or could have imagined in his wildest of thoughts.

That evening Harrod met Guruji again and told him everything that had transpired. He also told Guruji about what he thought were the lessons he had learnt from it.

With Guruji's presence, there was a strange light that illuminated any place he visited. Wherever he stepped, everything gave its way and here was Guruji to guide Harrod in understand the meaning of life and beyond and what destiny lay ahead for him.

Guruji explained, "Look at it this way, Harrod. You came to me from an unfamiliar environment, but settled well here since somewhere in your mind you knew, why you were coming to me. But some people do not know or realize why they have walked the distance in life, and then when destiny does something with them or takes charge, they stop dead in their tracks. Their life seems to stop in the middle of the road.

It is the same with the fishes. They did not know that one fish would leave them so suddenly, and they did not know why they were being transferred to the bucket. So, they jumped when you went to catch them. But when you gave the last one some time, it realized there you were in no hurry to catch it, and it gave way for you to hold it in your net.

There is nothing which we must do in haste. In haste, we are bound to make mistakes. In haste, we will falter, in haste, we will make others suffer and in haste, we will suffer ourselves. But when we provide the required time to ourselves, we will get our work done properly and so in the process will also be able to keep others happy. The fishes are just examples of what we do in our everyday lives, but they help teach us the essence of life.

When we treat every environment which we encounter on our path as our destiny and make it a part of our lives, we will enjoy being there. But when we treat the different environments with scepticism, we do more than harm to ourselves. In doubt and suspicion, our thoughts get shattered when we encounter something different from what we expected out of it and our life derails.

The fishes took very little time to adjust to the bucket of water as they understood fast about their temporary home. But as soon as you went to put them back into the bowl, they jumped into your net. They did not know why you were doing it but knew that you were not throwing them away and would put them in a better place. When you put them back in the bowl, you found them bubbling back with the same energy that they were in before. You found that their old thoughts had got washed away and fresh life breathed into them once again.

Similarly, all other beings on earth must learn to recharge their energies, which they have exhausted while fighting their destinies in life. The energy lies at the core of every being. We need to pull it out and use it for our well-being.

If you were to take the example of our planet Earth, you find that apart from supporting life, the earth also breathes life inside it. It is because of the planet that we also have life in us, while we support hundreds and thousands of other living organisms along with us. With whatever we do on and with mother Earth, the planet keeps on reinventing and revitalizing itself by moving earth and water. It displaces and replaces whatever we have taken from it. The core of the earth which burns in ourselves also is the reason we are living, similar to this planet. Just as the earth gets back its energies, similarly we also do, to revitalize ourselves and our souls.

Our soul does not rest, we do. Our soul does not lie, we do. We must be able to learn from our soul to support the lifeline of this entire system that comprises our mind, body and the universe."

Guruji got up, smiled at Harrod once, and then left for the day.

Harrod had his dinner as usual and then went back to his cottage.

It was time for Harrod to go to sleep. In his dreams, too, he saw the fishes making contact with him and thanking him for the constant interactions. He was almost obsessed with the fishes. With what was happening so vigorously inside his mind, a doctor could have told him to get psychiatric help. There were huge dunes and waves which had been created inside it. But here he was, simply hypnotized and mesmerized with the activities of the fishes and Guruji, and what they had taught him in the last few days of his life would become the support system during his lifetime.

But just as Guruji had pointed out earlier, Harrod knew very well that the fishes were there, only to help him understand the deeper meanings of life. Not that they were his only source, but certainly they had become his crutch in the last few days for understanding the deeper meaning of life. He had never thought that this would happen to him through the help of this fine medium - the fishes. He was learning to appreciate the true nature of his body's and nature's soul with much more intricacy.

That night he once again sat down next to his bed, took out his diary and wrote:

The Power of God

I resolved to ask

Just one question.

What is life?

I visited the temples,

The graveyards,

But ne'er could answer.

I waited,

For my life

To undergo

Turmoils and torments,

And peaceful, placid sails,

But still failed.

Could it be

Patience, strength, knowledge,

Or experience!

Or simply

A phase of beings!

Beginning with life,

Terminating with death,

For a test!

Whatever it is,

I have come,

Not to bathe

In bleeding wounds,

Not to suicide,

Not to be dismayed.

But to live,

To fulfil my aim,

Become frazzled,

But still

Face the challenge,

And attain my destiny,

Never resting

Till the end.

THE CONNECTIVITY BETWEEN ALL OF US

22

On the entire twenty-third day, Harrod was very excited and waited for the night to arrive. Although he had visited the fishes in the morning, completed his prayers, gone through his daily chores as usual, each moment his thoughts were glued to the words that Guruji had spoken, "you must come to me at midnight, when the world is asleep. I will wait for you in this temple. There is something more important that you must know." Millions of electric currents were rushing inside his brains to understand the surprise which Guruji had laid for him. He could not comprehend Guruji's reason for calling him during midnight to the temple. This was the only time that Guruji wanted Harrod alone in the temple and that too during midnight. What had Guruji planned for him?

His tensions were mounting as minutes and hours passed by; he could not sleep or do anything during the entire day, ate very little and was walked up and down in the ashram through the day with no other purpose, but the wish to meet Guruji during that night and learn something extraordinary from him.

Finally, after dinner, he sat in his cottage for some time, then came out and looked out at the open dark sky with millions of stars shining over him and where nothing else could be seen except the darkness between them. The entire ashram lights were out. The only light which came from a million light-years away was that from the distant stars. He wondered how humankind could even see the stars that shone from so far away, while on the planet, we could not even see beyond a certain distance. But night seemed to give man the power to see into space and into objects that were way beyond his reach. How could the power of the eyes change at night? How had the stars become so bright that their light could travel millions of light-years and reach earth from so far away and that too, from different constellations? During the day the only distant object that he could see was the sun with its full brightness and glory. But he could not look into the eyes of the sun because of its extreme heat and brightness. With the stars, he could. These were miraculous thoughts for him. Science had explained facts, but now they seemed irrelevant. It had opened new vistas for Harrod. He was not a scientist, but Harrod knew almost everything about the principle of science, but still could not explain how humans could be capable of creating similar objects of magic just like nature does.

Time passed as Harrod kept on looking at the open dark sky and somehow forgot about what Guruji had asked him to do. When he finally realized, it was nearing midnight. He quickly got up, washed his face and left for the temple. He did not know about the surprise which lay there for him.

When Harrod entered the temple, it was pitch dark. He did not know if the fishes were still swimming in the bowl. As he came near the temple, the doors opened for him automatically and when he had entered it, the doors closed automatically behind him, just as they had opened. All this was quite eerie for him, but Harrod knew it was Guruji who was in command there. Harrod softly said, "Guruji!"

There was no answer. The silence was deafening. But Harrod had by now learnt to counter silence, through what Guruji had taught him about concentration and by maintaining the inner silence while chanting the AUM mantra. He knew there was nothing to be afraid of now, and Guruji had certainly laid something important for him in all this.

A voice seemed to come from nowhere.

"Harrod, please sit down with your legs folded, hand put together and concentrate on what you are about to see," the voice said. The voice was thick, smooth and divine. Harrod could not recognize the voice as that of Guruji, but he knew somewhere that Guruji's soul was in it.

A small light appeared from the tiny hole on top of the temple and it came directly on the turban worn by Guruji. The white turban came to life. It was the same light that came into the temple during the day when Guruji was there and which Harrod had seen on his first visit to the temple. Harrod could see Guruji sitting in front of him with his eyes closed in an upright posture. In a split second, Guruji's turban unravelled and Guruji stood up from his sitting posture. For Harrod, it was just like a science fiction movie unravelling before him.

Guruji spoke, "Harrod, your journey in the first cycle stops tonight. From tomorrow you will step into your second cycle. You are a fast learner and have learnt the lessons of life fast here. Since you have been jotting down whatever I have been teaching, you will continue to remember everything. You will take the lessons you have learnt here, to other people after you complete all the cycles. But tonight, you will learn some extreme truths which will shake you and make you aware of your existence. Also, what I am going to reveal tonight, will only be for your eyes. No other person here in this temple, have been provided with this insight and therefore you must keep this to yourself only. I say this as you are the chosen one." Guruji's voice echoed in the temple.

Guruji continued, "Tonight you will learn how we are eternally connected with the universe. Tonight, you will learn how you too, can get the light burning inside you for periods beyond this life. Come with me to the journey of self-revelation."

No sooner had Guruji spoken, than the light coming into the temple through the tiny hole became brighter. Guruji held up his arms and prayed to the force which had given life to every single living thing in this universe. Suddenly there was a whiff of breeze inside the temple. The doors were closed, but still; the breeze came from somewhere which Harrod could not understand. Harrod had goosebumps on his entire body and he felt the shiver run through his spine.

The breeze started circling beneath the temple dome, slowly at first. By this time, Guruji's white turban had fallen. The fishbowl was now visible to Harrod, and he could see it rise above the wooden stilts that were once holding it. It was as though some external force or magnet was hauling the fishbowl. The fishes inside the bowl were circling inside the water with greater velocity.

With the increase in the power of the breeze inside the temple, the water inside the bowl had also started moving in circles. But Harrod was not moving. He stood there watching with utter disbelief at what was transpiring inside the closed doors of the temple.

The speed with which the fishes were circling inside the bowl was also increasing and after some time, with the breeze turning into a kind of cyclone, not imagined in the craziest thoughts of his mind, Harrod had lost sight of the fishes. The water in the bowl turned white, and the fishes had vanished. All the while, the light grew more and more intense.

While Harrod was still concentrating on the bowl, Guruji's body was turning into something which Harrod could never have imagined in his wildest of dreams. He saw the wind tearing into Guruji's body and shearing it. Slowly and magically, Guruji's body was disintegrating into smaller fragments. Guruji's white clothes and turban were now flying inside the temple in a circular format.

With the powering sound of the wind, it was becoming deafening for Harrod to continue watching all this. He was so terrified that he wanted to run out of the temple, but the thought of Guruji wanting him to understand something beyond what he had seen, kept him staring at the miraculous show. He gathered all his wits and courage and kept following the divine show.

Next to him and at the centre of the room, the bowl had risen above in the air and was getting bigger and larger.

After attaining a large enough size, it stopped expanding further. He could now see the fishes and water swirling inside it. Despite this, it was beyond Harrod's understanding of what was going on.

Just when the bowl had grown to its maximum size, next to it other round-shaped bodies appeared from nowhere and started circling the fishbowl. Everything in the room was changing into objects which had no meaning till then. Everything was happening so fast, yet so meticulously, that there was something that had a far greater meaning than life itself.

Guruji's sheared body also lifted from where he was, and then the shredded parts of his body started wrapping themselves onto the large fishbowl. It was a most unusual scene. The white turban and other clothes of his body were still circling in the open space. Just when all this was happening, at the far corner of the room, Harrod realized there was something else taking place. Small shiny objects were appearing in the darkness surrounding it.

When all this was happening, here was Guruji's body fully wrapped around the fishbowl and his body parts replaced that of the surface of the fishbowl. His tough bones were making rugged shapes on the fishbowl. His veins were opening up and getting strewn and tying themselves on its surface. They were all taking different shapes. The nerves had entered the core of the fishbowl and were centring in it. The hair of Guruji's body was all over the surface of the bowl.

While all this was happening, the water in the fishbowl kept swirling, then gathered itself all around Guruji's body and got placed in all those areas where Guruji's body had not covered it. But the fishes kept swimming wherever the water was getting diverted to.

The fishbowl was fast-changing its content. Now every part of Guruji's body had covered the bowl. Guruji had become the soul of the bowl by now. Harrod was now getting the feeling of recognizing what was happening. The bowl had transformed into the shape of a planet. But which one? Guruji's body was displaying a different picture of the planet.

Guruji's bones had by now formed shapes of mountains and rugged plains, his hair represented shrubs and trees, the veins of the body had changed into rivers, his organs had become the motors that drive the planet's ecological system, the heat of the body had accumulated itself into the central zone along with the brains and was glowing inside displaying the power of the heat inside. The place where Guruji's body did not have hair turned into arid land and deserts. The rest of the body parts had converted into important parts of the planet earth. Minerals of the body all converged with the body and formed part of the upper crust. The body oil became a part of one layer, which made the earth run itself. Every part of Guruji's body displayed its part on the planet Earth by then.

While Harrod watched this amazing feat taking place in front of his eyes, Guruji's clothes had taken the shape of a large white pathway on top and Harrod concluded it to be the Milky Way which he had read and seen pictures about. The bright lights he had seen at the corner turned into stars at a distance, the other objects which had appeared next to the bowl, had turned into the other planets and satellites of the solar system.

And as all this was happening, a bright light which formed part of Guruji's body and provided Guruji with his life, came out and travelled across the room at an extraordinary speed and then suddenly became the nerve centre of the place and lit so brightly that Harrod got blindfolded. This Harrod imagined being the sun. The whole solar system was here before his eyes balancing each other, rotating or revolving as per their destined ways.

Harrod stood still at the centre of the temple, mesmerized by what he had just seen. It was as though he was standing in deep space and formed an integral part of the great universe. The winds that had started in the beginning and which circled in the entire temple slowed down and were now only blowing gently over the fishbowl, providing an atmosphere to it. All the rest of the bodies depicting the other planets were on the journey around the sun, which provided light to the entire solar system.

It was as if Harrod had just watched a dream and wanted to imagine that it was too hard to believe. He was on earth but felt like being in deep space. He pinched himself and felt the pinch. He could still see what he had just experienced. Guruji was nowhere to be seen and in his place and the place of the fishbowl stood planet Earth, in its full glory around the sun. The fishes were still part of the system but represented life on earth now.

Just when Harrod was watching all this, there was a sudden pin-drop silence in the temple. There were no words for Harrod now. Everything that Harrod had desired till now seemed to have got wiped off his dream screen. He felt and understood the power of the system that ruled us. He felt he was a part of the system that God had produced for everyone. But he also recognized the greatness of what was a superb creation which God had put in place. The entire universe was a replication of each thing in different forms, and humans were the supreme beings who represented every aspect of the universe themselves.

There was darkness in the entire temple, but Harrod could still see everything clearly as if he was watching the night sky and the stars, the moon could be seen even when the entire place was dark. Harrod could understand the meaning of light and darkness. Every part of his life had a bright side and a dark side to it, just as the universe and just as the planet earth. He could understand the significance of the planets around the fishbowl. Every portion of the solar system was connected to immaculately. Each planet depended on the others. Each planet had a special effect on the other. Similar to the solar system, was the human body.

If Harrod's body represented the planet earth, so did it represent the solar system and so did it represent the universe? Just as his body had an inner glowing heat which kept him alive, the earth too had an inner heat which kept it alive and so did the solar system had an inner light in the sun's form which kept the planets alive and similarly there were other larger heat sources which kept the solar system alive and so forth.

There was no record of the time when Harrod was watching all this and he did not have the slightest idea how much time had passed since he had got inside the temple, but it appeared hours had passed by.

As Harrod was thinking about all this, suddenly the universe that he had just seen disappeared and there was darkness once again in the temple. In the centre was the fishbowl once again, and Guruji in his meditation was seated there. Guruji opened his eyes, and the temple got illuminated. Harrod could see the fishes swimming in the fishbowl as usual, and Guruji was looking as charming and divine as ever.

Harrod sat still, absolutely stunned by what he had seen. He could not believe his eyes. Had he just seen God and his miracles? Was he blessed with the powers to see the extraordinary? Had he been given certain special powers by which only he could have seen the wonder that he had just witnessed?

Guruji finally spoke. "Harrod, by now you must have known what I wanted to teach you. You have correctly interpreted whatever you have seen. I have seen you think rationally. But I must still tell you certain things that you must know and for which there are questions still in your mind.

You are indeed the chosen one since you have seen what many others have not and you have experienced something extraordinary that others have not. You have been the chosen one since I know you will show the world the correct path to travel upon. My work is to identify people who would spread the word across and so I choose different people from time to time and assign them to work in this world in different ways. You are one of them. But I assign each one a distinct set of work.

If you have seen the ashram properly, there are few disciples here, but I have picked each one who has come here, as he was destined to be here. Every disciple here has a separate mission in life, and they are in this place to recognize it and work towards their goal. But they all will spread the word of the almighty, about our existence in life and help people understand their purpose and choose the correct path in life.

I have chosen you since you are the right one. But you must prove this by going through all the cycles which I explained to you when you were first here. Otherwise, all this will go to waste and you will forget everything and become a commoner once again. Since you are destined to cover the cycles, you must and sincerely work towards it. One day you will attain all your inner powers and then you will do things that no one else can. For all this, your life must be as simple as possible. You must enjoy the simplicity and you must trust and rely on your faculties."

Guruji continued, "Let me once again take you to the scene which you just witnessed. You saw how living beings are a minor representation of the universe, the solar system, and the earth. We must all look into ourselves and we will find everything that we need to understand about the universe.

The universe is a larger representation of the galaxy, and the galaxy is a larger representation of the solar system. The solar system is a larger representation of the earth. Similarly, the earth is a larger representation of the life forms on it, and the living organisms on the planet are the smallest representation of the earth and so forth. From where we stand, there are things larger than us and there are organisms much smaller than us. Within us also, as science has already proved, are cells, molecules, atoms, protons, neutrons, electrons, and the world keeps on getting smaller and we can only understand till we can fathom into it. On both sides, beyond everything that we can fathom, is only space. Everything is connected so perfectly. Without the smallest, there will be no greatest.

If you were to examine what you have learned from this, you will see a lot more reasoning. Since we represent the earth, what we do with ourselves affects the Earth. What we do with Earth will affect the solar system. What we do with the solar system will affect the universe. It is slow but a definite effect of our actions, for which the universe will pay a price and so will we.

What will happen if we keep on destroying our values? By doing so, we will destroy the basis of what our planet stands on - its ecological system. When we think about our short-term gains, we do things that are detrimental to the system on which Earth stands. The planet Earth tries to correct itself by bringing in typhoons, earthquakes, storms, tidal waves, volcanic eruptions, incessant rains, just as our body has built-in mechanisms to treat the various forms of sufferings that we are subject to from time to time. We treat our body with unwanted food and we treat our body with unwanted drugs; we treat our mind with unwanted thoughts, and we treat our soul with unwanted values in life. Just as the earth has volcanic eruptions, earthquakes and other mishaps, our body also reacts with fever, boils on the skin, different diseases - internal and external, long and short, when we consume contaminated food, water, air or thoughts. Our body reacts to our unwanted actions during our life by giving us different hardships, which become part of our life or culminate into sufferings at the end of our life.

If you were to take the life of a smoker and talk to him, you will see most of the time, he will keep telling you that nothing happens to him when he smokes. But if he takes a pause, he will face hardships in the form of diseases which will teach him not to smoke again or in the form of an uncontrollable urge to have it again. If he does not quit, he faces hardships at the end of his life through sufferings that torment him mentally and physically because of his habit. This is bound to happen. The body will try to correct itself and, in the process, torment him. Similar to the smoker is our planet. When you fill it up with smoke and pollutants, the planet will correct itself and, in the process, bring about the different weather correction features to counter this. If the planet cannot bear, it will create such hardships, which will either limit or destroy life completely. This is bound to happen.

Destiny has chalked itself for this planet and if we play with it, it will automatically put the process in its right flow, thereby creating severe hurdles for all of us. This is just an example of what could happen in one of the given circumstances, and every such example will show you that you should first respect the purity of what has been created for you and given to you in abundance.

Treat everything on the planet and the universe with respect. Don't play around for individual gains, but play for collective gains of the universal truth at large. The universal truth is that we exist because we are destined to be, and destiny will leave no stone unturned to keep the system moving as it is destined to do so. But, if there is something due to which it can't keep the system moving on, it will allow the system to destroy itself and recreate everything anew."

Guruji kept on guiding, "You must complete the other cycles now and you will see what destiny has in store for you. Before you teach the truth to the entire world, come back to me after you have completed all the cycles. During all the cycles, you will find my support whenever you remember me, but you must never lose faith in yourself because above all the faith that we all have in different things including different Gods, faith in ourselves is of utmost necessity as the supreme force lies only within us. Faith in ourselves with true value systems will lead us to success and near the supreme one, and we will ultimately get connected and integrated with the forces of nature, which is what destiny is all about."

With these words, and with the promise that they would meet again, Guruji vanished into thin air in front of Harrod. The temple was there, but there was no fishbowl, as he had seen during the past few days. The temple was empty. Was it a big dream that Harrod had just witnessed? Harrod knew everything would be true till he believed it to be so, and Guruji had told him exactly that.

Harrod came out of the temple shocked and bewildered. On reaching his cottage, he checked the time. For him, it seemed as if hours had passed, but when he saw the time, it left him speechless. The time was still midnight. How could this be possible? He had watched the entire movie, and surely it had taken time. What then was the reason for time not moving?

Without losing a moment, Harrod sat down and closed his eyes and then remembered Guruji. Guruji was there in his thoughts and answered his question.

Guruji said, "Harrod, you have just travelled through time during the last few moments. That is why there is a difference between the time that you see in your watch and the eternal time. The time that you see here on this planet is just a fraction of the time that rules the universe. So, it must have seemed hours to you when you saw the unfolding of the truth, but in reality, it was a fraction of a second of the universal timeline. So now you still see things as if nothing happened. You have just traversed the universal time."

Guruji's face vanished from Harrod's site and he slowly opened his eyes, truth glaring at him. Time was a measurement he learnt all his life and here was Guruji telling him about this time which was only a fraction of the universal time. How was the universe running then, and where and how were we fitting into it? How was the universe powered and from which turbines were so much power being generated that time was also getting fractioned?

That night Harrod had a fantastic experience, an experience of a lifetime. He had to treasure every moment. If the last few days could teach Harrod such extraordinary things, then what would happen during and after the completion of the other three cycles?

It was something Harrod had to wait for.

He wrote his last words before setting off on the journey to his next cycle.

The Ultimate

The darkness has to fall,

The tremors have to shake.

This catastrophe

Will level cities.

Old persons, infants, children

And stray visitors,

Will fall,

In the hail of random

Bullets and bombs.

And!

There will be victims in all.

They will get

Burned, stabbed, hacked

And probably decapitated.

Still the impact

Of violent incidents,

Will not reveal

The chronicle of deaths.

But! The end of an era.

The following Day Harrod took Guruji's blessings and left the ashram in search of the remaining 3 cycles which would empower and transform his life.

About the Author

Apart from being an author himself, Neeraj Singhvi is a life transformation coach, business owner and marketing strategist with 25+ years of hardcore corporate exposure. Neeraj Singhvi is a management graduate and a qualified Management Accountant. He has written books like "Temple of Destiny", "Write a Million Dollar Book in 10 Days" and is also co-author of "Adventures into the Unknown" and "Transformusings". He is an avid podcaster and blogger whose passion is writing. His books are available on all online portals. Follow him on:

Twitter @neeraj101

Facebook @author.neeraj.singhvi

Buy his other books here:

Write a Million Dollar Book in 10 days:

Amazon.com: https://amz.run/4Lr8

Amazon.in: https://amz.run/4Lr9

Adventures into the Unknown:

Lulu.com: https://bit.ly/2RDuCsh

Transformusings:

Amazon.com: https://amzn.to/3iJBLDp

Amazon.in: https://amzn.to/3hFd2ic

Books by the author

Notes

Write about any ideas or thoughts you get...

If you would like to find out more about yourself and empower yourself to take on the world, take this lovely 2-minute 30-day course, created just for you.

REGISTER HERE

https://bit.ly/2OtAzJX

For interacting with the author, please send in your comments at:
qsortsindia@gmail.com
www.qsortsindia.com